What Are You Really Eating?

Hay House Titles of Related Interest

The Allergy Exclusion Diet:
The 28-Day Plan to Solve Your Food Intolerances,
by Jill Carter and Alison Edwards

Eating in the Light:
Making the Switch to Vegetarianism on Your Spiritual Path,
by Doreen Virtue, Ph.D., and Becky Prelitz, M.F.T., R.D.

The Herbal Detox Plan:
The Revolutionary Way to Cleanse and Revive Your Body,
by Xandria Williams

The Natural Nutrition No-Cook Book:
Delicious Food for YOU . . . and Your PETS!,
by Kymythy R. Schultze

To Serve with Love:
Simple, Scrumptious Meals from the Skinny to the Sinful,
by Carnie Wilson, with Cindy Pearlman

Vegetarian Meals for People-on-the-Go,
by Vimala Rodgers

Wheat-Free, Worry-Free:
The Art of Happy, Healthy, Gluten-Free Living,
by Danna Korn

* * *

All of the above are available at your
local bookstore, or may be ordered by visiting:

Hay House USA: **www.hayhouse.com**
Hay House Australia: **www.hayhouse.com.au**
Hay House UK: **www.hayhouse.co.uk**
Hay House South Africa: **orders@psdprom.co.za**

What Are You Really Eating?

How to Become Label Savvy

613.2

Amanda Ursell

HAY HOUSE, INC.
Carlsbad, California
London • Sydney • Johannesburg
Vancouver • Hong Kong

Copyright © 2005 by Amanda Ursell

Published and distributed in the United States by: Hay House, Inc.,
P.O. Box 5100, Carlsbad, CA 92018-5100 • *Phone:* (760) 431-
7695 or (800) 654-5126 • *Fax:* (760) 431-6948 or (800) 650-5115
• www.hayhouse.com • *Published and distributed in Australia by:*
Hay House Australia Pty. Ltd., 18/36 Ralph St., Alexandria NSW
2015 • *Phone:* 612-9669-4299 • *Fax:* 612-9669-4144 • www.
hayhouse.com.au • *Published and distributed in the United Kingdom by:* Hay House UK, Ltd. • Unit 62, Canalot Studios • 222
Kensal Rd., London W10 5BN • *Phone:* 44-20-8962-1230 • *Fax:*
44-20-8962-1239 • www.hayhouse.co.uk • *Published and distributed in the Republic of South Africa by:* Hay House SA (Pty), Ltd.,
P.O. Box 990, Witkoppen 2068 • *Phone/Fax:* 27-11-706-6612 •
orders@psdprom.co.za • *Distributed in Canada by:* Raincoast •
9050 Shaughnessy St., Vancouver, B.C. V6P 6E5 • *Phone:* (604)
323-7100 • *Fax:* (604) 323-2600

Editorial supervision: Jill Kramer • *Design:* Tricia Breidenthal

Library of Congress Control Number: 2005927002

ISBN 13: 978-1-4019-0704-4
ISBN 10: 1-4019-0704-0

08 07 06 05   4 3 2 1
1st printing, October 2005

Printed in the United States of America

Contents

Chapter 1: Getting Label Savvy...................1

Chapter 2: Nutrition Labels.......................35

Chapter 3: Nutrition Claims......................67

Chapter 4: Health Claims..........................85

Chapter 5: Fresh, Natural, and Lactose-Free . . . What Do These Terms Mean? 117

Chapter 6: Symbols and Logos 131

Chapter 7: Children's Food 147

Chapter 8: Organic Food 169

Chapter 9: Genetically Modified Food.....185

Chapter 10: Functional Food 195

Chapter 11: Additives 219

Resource Guide 235

Acknowledgments 241

About the Author 243

For Gérald

Chapter 1

Getting Label Savvy

If you've ever felt confused by the amount of information crammed onto a food label, you aren't alone, and this is definitely the book for you! I'll let you in on a secret: I'm a nutritionist, and until I sat down to write this, even I was occasionally bewildered by some of the things I saw at the grocery store.

For example, when you're looking at a carton covered in pictures of fruit, you could be forgiven for thinking that the drink inside of it contains significant amounts of juice from that fruit. Not necessarily. In reality, "fruit drinks" are often no more than flavored water that's artificially colored, packed with added sugars, and consisting of no more than 5 percent juice. The moral is not to be seduced by what you see at first glance, but to instead read the fine print—and this book will teach you how.

Why Do Labels Exist?

When trying to make sense of what you're looking at, it's first important to understand that labels are there for two main reasons. First, from a practical point of view, they tell you the name of what you've picked up, which ingredients it's made from, its weight, and where it comes from.

But labels are also there to encourage you to buy the product. They're like miniature ads for what's inside the packaging, so it's their job to look as attractive and seductive as possible. The food companies' designers do this by using bright colors and pictures, clever graphics, and (increasingly these days) by highlighting the products' nutritional and health credentials.

The labels aren't allowed to deliberately mislead us (doing so is actually illegal), but it's vital to be aware that manufacturers are obviously going to make the most of their products' good points while not drawing attention to their less-than-virtuous ones. It's really no different from any of us just making the most of our own assets.

Making the Most of Themselves

I've always thought that labels are a bit like clothes and cosmetics. We buy outfits that suit us and enhance our appearance in ways that bring out our good points. In other words, if you have Julia-Roberts-type legs or a nipped-in waist like Jennifer Lopez, it makes sense to show off these assets. Similarly, if the makers of certain cookies, for example, know that the product is high in fiber, they'll want to tell you this on the label.

They'd be a bit crazy, however, to draw your attention to the fact that the cookies are also packed with fat, sugar, and salt. Not highlighting these points (which are obviously going to deter many customers from buying the snack) is like not wearing something that you know is going to accentuate those parts of your body that you'd rather play down. That is, just as most of us know how to dress to hide our flaws, manufacturers know how to disguise the worst features of their products in order show the item in the most appealing light.

You can't blame them. They're in the business of selling food, after all, and want you to buy as much as possible. But understanding why and how they try to make that sale is important if you really want to know the nitty-gritty of what you're eating.

Going Back to Basics

With many tens of thousands of types of food and drink now on sale in an average supermarket, learning how to read a label will help put you in charge of your cart when you're shopping and allow you to make informed choices about what you and your family eat and drink.

My 97-year-old grandmother tells me that in her day, all food shopping involved a daily trip to the local stores. She went to the baker for fresh bread made from scratch, to the produce stand where she popped carrots into a trusty string bag, and to the butcher for a hand-wrapped favorite cut of meat that was just enough for that night's dinner.

Today, we lead busy lives, which means that we tend to do all of our shopping in one weekly (or even monthly) trip, under one roof, in one supermarket. Our habits have changed: No longer do many of us walk around town to various specialized stores on a daily basis. Instead, we buy in bulk, and this means that most of the items we purchase have in some way been processed before appearing on the supermarket's shelves. And since these foods come in packets, boxes, cans, and bottles, it's just as well that, by law, they have to be marked. Consequently, labels have become a necessity.

This book will help you make sense of food labels and give you the chance to really understand what you're feeding yourself and those around you. The first step on that road is a quick overview of the requirements faced by today's manufacturers.

The Letter of the Law

Labels can come in all shapes, sizes, colors, and designs, but there are some things that must legally appear on them, including:

- The name of the food
- A list of ingredients
- The name and address of the manufacturer or packer
- The net weight
- The nutritional content

It's up to the Food and Drug Administration (FDA) to create and then enforce these laws so that as a customer, you can at least try to make informed choices about what you buy. Labels are also intended to let you know how to keep and prepare the product safely, and that producers are selling their food to you in an honest way.

It may seem hard to believe while wandering

around a grocery store, but there are eight major laws governing what appears on food labels:

1. The Federal Food, Drug, and Cosmetic Act: This is the main law that deals with food labeling in America, and it applies to all food and drink, with three exceptions: alcoholic beverages, meat, and poultry (such as chicken and turkey).

2. The Federal Meat Inspection Act

3. The Poultry Products Inspection Act

4. The Egg Products Inspection Act: Meat and poultry labeling falls under these umbrella acts that lay down strict laws governing how such items are handled and made into products like lunch meat. The Food Safety and Inspection Service (FSIS) of the U.S. Department of Agriculture enforces these particular laws.

5. The Fair Packaging and Labeling Act: This act applies to all food sold between states and makes sure that labeling is correct.

6. The Federal Trade Commission Act: This legislation controls the advertising of food sold between states. It means that manufacturers can't make outrageous claims in their promotional material.

7. The Federal Alcohol Administration Act: This law controls the labeling of most alcoholic beverages, such as distilled spirits and wine. It ensures that these products' packaging declares that they can impair your ability to drive a car or operate machinery, can increase the risk of birth defects if pregnant women consume them, and details of other health effects.

8. The Federal Tariff Act: And finally, with this act, you can be sure that what you buy has information in the most commonly used language in the U.S.: English!

Within these various acts are regulations that control what's allowed on nutrition labels and what health claims can be made. They state that it's illegal to mislead consumers as to the "nature or substance or quality of the food" through the use of words or pictures.

For example, it's a crime for a label to say that a bottle contains sunflower oil—or to imply that it does by showing lots of big sunflower plants—when in fact the bottle contains a mix of sunflower and other oils.

It's also illegal to "pad" foods, such as adding cheaper cuts of meat to a dish marked as containing premium steak; or for manufacturers not to declare that a food such as shrimp, which appears fresh from the fish counter, has been previously frozen.

Misinformation is at best bad news, because you end up paying more for cheaper versions of a product, and at worst, a potential danger to your health. If, for example, a food has been filled with flour to increase its volume and you suffer from gluten intolerance, then you could have an adverse reaction. This is one of the many reasons that it's crucial for labels to be truthful, and why all these laws have been put into place.

The key to tackling your shopping now and in the future is first figuring out how to read the label. Then, perhaps most important, learn how to interpret it. That means understanding, on the one hand, the information that manufacturers have to tell you by law; and on the other, how they try to sway you to buy their products rather than a competitor's. Let's take a look at the basic components of a label so that you'll have a framework for the more specific information that fills the rest of this book.

The Big Picture

One way to get a good idea of what goes into each and every item in the grocery store is to imagine designing a product of your own. Let's say that you've just created your own line of pasta sauces, which you've decided to call "Getting Saucy." (Okay, it's a terrible name, but bear with me!) The first creation in your brand is a great spicy sauce for pouring over pasta.

You can't just make the sauce, throw it in a bottle, call a supermarket, and ask them to put it on their shelves. One of the first things you'll have to do is design a label, and as I outlined, there's a certain amount of information that U.S. laws absolutely insist that you put on it.

The Name

To begin with, you'll need to decide on the name—also called, rather formally, the "statement of identity." How about "Getting Saucy—The Spicy Tomato One"? Whatever name you choose needs to go on what's known as the "principal display panel," which is what's most visible to customers when it's sitting on the shelf.

Because the word *tomato* has been mentioned in the name of the product, the percentage of tomatoes in the sauce must be provided on the principal display panel. (The same would be true if you were designing a label for fish sticks: You'd need to state how much fish is actually in the sticks.)

You'll also have to tell your customers if your sauce is fresh or has undergone any special type of treatment (such as ultra-heat treatment); or if it's been concentrated, smoked, pasteurized, canned, frozen, dried, or freeze-dried.

The idea is that this information will help eliminate misrepresentation and provide insight into the best way to store it. For example, if the principal display panel of frozen-fish sticks says the word *frozen,* you'll assume that you, too, have to keep them in the freezer before using.

But back to your pasta sauce: On this main section of the label, you'll also need to give the net quantity of sauce in the jar—in other words, the amount that your customers can expect to find inside.

There's a specific way in which this information must be provided. In the case of solid foods, it must be given in pounds and ounces. If you were making a spicy-tomato soup instead of a pasta sauce, because the soup is more fluid, the net quantity would be expressed in terms of gallons, quarts, or pints and fluid ounces. This also holds true for other liquids such as fruit juice.

In fact, U.S. law also requires net contents to be given in metric units, although in truth, this isn't always enforced.

What's in It?

Immediately to the right of the principal display panel, you'll need to give your customers more details about what they're buying in the "information panel."

First, make sure that there's a list of ingredients that you've used to make your new sauce. For example, it could be: salt, onions, basil, garlic, tomatoes, pepper, and chilis. You'll also have to list any additives, such as preservatives or colors.

But you can't just write it all down in any old order. You need to display them clearly, visibly, and in order of descending weight (including any water). In other words, the first item is the one that the product contains the most of. So your list might look like this: "Ingredients: tomatoes, water, onions, garlic, basil, chilis, salt, pepper."

When to Use By

Technically called the "durability indication," you may be more familiar with terms such as "shelf-life dating" or simply "use-by date"—that is, the date by which your customers need to use the tomato sauce. Telling them how to store the product to ensure that it's at its best when eaten is also useful. For example, you could say, "Store in the refrigerator and use within two days of opening."

Who You Are

Any packaged food or drink sold in the United States must give the name and place of business of the U.S. manufacturer, packer, or distributor. This party is known as the "responsible agent." This means that customers can contact you if they have a complaint, comment, query, or just want to write to tell you what a fabulous sauce you've concocted! You must provide the name of the responsible agent with their address, including the street, city, state, and zip code.

Special Instructions

As if that isn't enough data to have to squeeze onto the information panel, you'll also need to let your customers know if there are any special things they have to do in order to use the product. In the case of your sauce, there probably won't be anything unusual, although you do have to give the necessary instructions on how to use it. It may be completely obvious, but you'll still have to say something like this: "Empty contents into a saucepan, warm on medium heat for five minutes while stirring constantly, then pour over freshly cooked and drained pasta."

Nutrition Information

In the U.S, virtually all foods must by law provide customers with nutrition information, which appears in the "nutrition facts" panel. The only exceptions that don't have to carry this detail are raw products, such as fresh fruits or vegetables and fresh cuts of meat; and in some cases, small businesses are also exempt from supplying it on their products. See Chapter 2 to find out more about nutrition labeling.

Those are the basics that you'll find on every product. Now that you have a general sense of what you're looking for, let's go into more detail about each of these components, beginning with some important definitions.

Defining Our Terms

As I mentioned, along with the name in the principal display panel, you also need to include information about proper storage and descriptive terms such as *pasteurized, canned, frozen,* or *dried.* These words have specific meanings and parameters when used on a label:

- **Fresh:** This term can only be used when the food hasn't been subjected to any form of heat or chemical processing, such as freshly squeezed orange juice.

- **Frozen:** This word must be prominently displayed. It should help stop less scrupulous manufacturers from thawing out frozen foods, such as fish, and then trying to sell them as "fresh." It also gives customers a good indication that the product needs to be stored frozen once at home.

- **Frozen Fresh:** Foods that were quickly frozen while still fresh may be labeled with either this term or "fresh frozen."

- **Canned:** To qualify as being a canned food, the product must have been hermetically sealed and processed by heat to prevent insects, bacteria, and the like from growing and spoiling the food inside. Foods in metal containers that are obviously canned don't need to actually say so on the label. But those that have undergone the hermetic sealing and heat treatment, and are in bottles or jars that could otherwise appear fresh, do need to be marked "canned." It may sound a bit bizarre to call something canned when it's in a bottle, but that's the law.

- **Dried or dehydrated:** Unless the food has obviously been dried (such as raisins), it must carry one of these two descriptions so that customers are in no doubt as to the processing it has undergone.

- **Freeze-dried:** If a food has undergone the freeze-dry technique, then as a manufacturer, you can just use the word *dried,* oddly enough, although the labeling laws prefer that you say freeze-dried.

- **Energy:** Lots of labels contain the word *energy.* Manufacturers presumably use it to imply that their food will help you feel more energetic and fight fatigue. It certainly looks and sounds compelling, but in fact, there's no proof that "energy" foods can do such things, beyond the fact that their calories are converted by your cells into fuel that powers them.

- **Comforting names:** Products bearing words such as "freshly prepared" or "natural" tend to make shoppers feel cozy and warm—but what do they actually mean? In some cases, not very much! In Chapter 5, you'll find out more about this issue.

When you know what's meant by these basic terms, it's easier to decipher one of the most commonly examined components of a food label: the ingredient list.

What's Inside?

The block of text telling you what's in the food you're eating can be even more complex than it first appears—and that's saying something! But take comfort in the fact that you're already familiar with the two most important rules about this part of a label:

1. Items are put in their weight-descending order at the time the product is being prepared.

2. Water is considered to be an ingredient, so it must be listed in order of its weight in the finished product.

But there's a lot more to it than that. Here are some lesser-known facts about that fine print on the side of the box (and the can and the bag):

*   When spices are added, they can be given their common name (such as basil or parsley) or can simply be listed as "spices."

*   If a natural flavoring like real vanilla is added, then the list of ingredients can say

"vanilla," "flavor," "flavoring," "natural flavor," or "natural flavoring."

- However, an ingredient that enhances flavor (such as monosodium glutamate) must
  definitely be given its proper commonly
  used name so that you're in no doubt of its
  presence.

- Flavors that come from artificial sources and
  are therefore not natural must be declared
  on the label as "artificial flavors."

- When it comes to colors, all of those
  approved by the FDA-certified-colors law
  must be listed and given either their complete or abbreviated names.

- If a product contains a mixture of colors,
  then the label must state "artificial colors."

- Noncertified colors must be given in the
  form of their specific common name. Some
  examples are "caramel coloring," "artificial
  color," "color added," or "artificial color
  added."

- When spices are used to give color—for example, saffron imparting a golden-yellow color to rice—the label must say either the specific ingredient name ("saffron") or "spice and coloring."

- Items added for a specific purpose are known technically as *functional ingredients,* and can be listed with either their name or function first. An example of such a substance is soy lecithin, which acts as an emulsifier to keep oil and water together in a food like a salad dressing so that it doesn't separate. In a case like this, the label can either say "soy lecithin (emulsifier)" or "emulsifier (soy lecithin)." Another example is "citric acid (acidifier)" or "acidifier (citric acid)."

- If it happens that a manufacturer may from time to time use different ingredients (for example, when leavening baked foods), it's legal to just say "stabilizing agents," and then list in parentheses the ones that may be being used. It might look like this: "stabilizing agents (mono and diglycerides, and/or guar gum)."

- When it comes to complex scientific ingredients, it's often useful to give the common
  name, followed by the scientific term in
  parentheses. For packaged rolls, for example, the list might say, "baking soda (sodium
  bicarbonate)."

- Many processed foods contain preservatives
  to stop them from going bad. The most
  ancient and commonly used are salt and
  vinegar. These days, lots of artificial ones are
  also available to food manufacturers. When
  these kinds of chemicals are added, the
  ingredient list must provide the name of the
  additive and its role. Here are a few common ones: "Ascorbic acid (to help retain
  color)," "Vitamin E (to prevent oxidation),"
  and "Sorbic acid (to maintain freshness)."

- Many manufactured foods have had milk
  protein called *caseinates* added to them.
  These may provide bulk or emulsify oils and
  water. Because some people actively try
  to avoid dairy, the label of a food containing this substance must say "caseinate (a
  milk derivative)" so that people can clearly
  understand that it's present.

- Protein hydrolysates are additives made
  from protein such as milk, meat, and soy.
  They have all kinds of roles in food processing, from adding flavor to helping stabilize
  foods and drinks. The FDA says that it's not
  enough for manufacturers just to list "protein hydrolysates." Instead, they must also
  say where these substances come from—for
  example, hydrolyzed meat or hydrolyzed
  soy protein.

- Irradiation of a main ingredient is considered to be a food additive by the FDA and
  must be declared on the ingredients list.

- The artificial sweetener aspartame, which
  has the brand name NutraSweet, contains
  an amino acid (a protein building block)
  called *phenylalanine.* A small minority of
  people have a condition called *phenylketon-
  uria* that means they're unable to digest it
  effectively. Because of this, all foods containing aspartame must carry a warning on the
  Information Panel saying, "Phenylketon-
  urics—contains phenylalanine."

All of these provisions are designed to keep you, as a consumer, safe and informed. To meet those goals with certain foods, however, requires even more stringent regulations.

Meat and Poultry

Most of the labeling requirements for meat and poultry are the same as the ones described above. However, the Food Safety and Inspections Act (which applies specifically to these items) demands that food labels be seen and approved before they're used. This means that if your hypothetical pasta sauce contained meat, its label would need approval before being allowed on your product. In the case of other foods (such as a straightforward creamy pasta sauce), no approval is needed.

Ingredients and Additives

The Food Safety and Inspections Act has detailed lists of permitted ingredients and additives, including anything from burgers to meatballs, from chicken nuggets to turkey bacon. The specific information is contained in a work called the *Labeling Policy Book.*

When a meat product (such as sausage) is part of another dish and contains lots of ingredients of its own, that sublist must be provided in parentheses. You can expect to see something like this: "Ingredients: sausage (pork, water, salt, spices, and sodium nitrite)."

To continue with the example, if the sausage contains other added ingredients that the manufacturer may alter from time to time, then these can be listed by declaring, "(may also contain sugar, lactic acid, and sodium ascorbate)."

Sources and Processing

Labeling requirements for meat and poultry foods aren't limited to the ingredients list. They also include information about where the items came from and what happened to them before they reached you.

These product labels are allowed to tell customers that they're free from certain ingredients. They can, for example, say "No pork" so that those who avoid this meat for religious reasons can clearly see that the item is okay for them to buy.

Many people prefer to buy meat and poultry that hasn't been treated with hormones. The manufacturer

can put "No hormones added" on the labels of pork
and poultry foods as long as it's followed by the statement: "Federal regulations prohibit the use of hormones." (See Chapter 8 for information on organic
food.)

For beef products, the same "No hormones
added" assertion can be made, as long as it can be
justified and doesn't need the federal-regulations
statement. Similarly, manufacturers can label their
products "No antibiotics," as long as they can prove
this to be the case.

Further along in the preparation process, when
meat that's been mechanically separated from bones
is used, the label must say "mechanically separated
beef" (or chicken, turkey, or whatever). And when
meat or poultry is cooked in a bag that contains un-
drained juices, the label must say so. It will carry
words such as "contains up to 5% solution."

When Is "Lean" Ground Beef
Not What It Seems?

As with all labeling, that of meat and poultry must
not be misleading or false in any way. The U.S Department of Agriculture tells manufacturers that in order

to be labeled as being "lean," all meat and poultry must contain no more than 10 percent fat by weight——except, that is, for ground beef. When it comes to this family favorite, there's a loophole that allows it to be labeled "lean" or even "extra lean," while containing up to 22.5 percent fat—which isn't very lean at all! This is a perfect example of needing to know the finer details of food labeling in order to get a clear understanding of what you're actually eating.

And just as meat and poultry have their special issues and concerns, so do foods from the plant kingdom.

Pesticides

When it comes to vegetables, fruit, and cereal crops (such as wheat and rice), the concern is not with hormones and antibiotics, but with residues of pesticides used during their growth, and chemicals present during storage to prevent spoilage or slow down the ripening process.

You'll be glad to know that the Environmental Protection Agency provides standards called "tolerances" for residues of such substances, and that government agencies test products and monitor levels in foods whether produced in the U.S. or imported from other countries. And if a food like a prepared salad has been processed using a specially permitted gas, then the container will tell you that it has been packed in a protective atmosphere.

If you don't like the idea of "tolerance" levels and prefer your food to have as few sprays as possible used in its production, then you'll probably be a fan of organic produce. The rules governing this designation mean that growers are open about any substances they've used and keep them to an absolute minimum. (See Chapter 8 for information on organic food.)

When Ingredients Don't Appear

Despite all of the rules and regulations, there are still some things that don't make it onto food labels. For example, when ingredients appear in tiny amounts and don't have a technical reason for being there, they're referred to as being "incidental" and don't need to be put on the label. These include:

- Ingredients that have been added and that served a purpose during production, but have no function in the final food or drink.

- Something put in during processing but removed before the final product is packaged and sold.

- Substances that may move into the item from the processing equipment of the packaging.

- Certain additives found in dairy products. Although they usually have to be listed, the law says that this isn't the case for artificial colorings, flavorings, and preservatives that are added to butter, cheese, and ice cream.

Having looked at the very tiniest traces that are too small to count, we're now going to move back out to look at the bigger picture. After all, not everything that you consume comes with a label.

Foods That Don't Need a List of Ingredients

If you'd decided to go into business selling fruit, vegetables, fresh fish, or eggs (rather than pasta sauces), then as long as you sold them whole and didn't peel or chop them up into pieces, you wouldn't have to bother with a label at all, let alone a list of ingredients. There are many other common-sense items in this category:

- A product made of a single ingredient, such as salt.

- Carbonated mineral water. As long as the bottle tells you somewhere that the water is carbonated, there's no need for a special little box saying "water and carbon dioxide."

- Food served in restaurants. (That is, unless a claim is made on the menu that it's fat-free, for instance.)

- Anything served for immediate consumption, or prepared in small establishments that will be eaten there (or somewhere else at a later date if the customer asks for a package to go).

- Food that's in a package with less than 12 inches of space (such as a pack of chewing gum), as long as nutritional information can be obtained should the customer wish to get it.

Even if you're not dealing with one of these items and you've read through the list of ingredients, there's still a lot more information on the label for you to process.

Where Does My Food Come From?

If a food has been imported into the U.S., then the country it came from must be put on the label in a way that can be easily read and isn't likely to peel or rub off. This information must be in English. If it's been imported and then repackaged once here, the new container must say "Imported from . . ." and give the country of origin.

Products containing ingredients from more than one nation are required to provide the details of all of these places, and all of this information must be put as close as possible to the name and address of the responsible agent.

What's in a Date?

Oddly enough, with the exception of milk and eggs, the law doesn't require manufacturers to supply the durability indication—when the product should be used by—in a specific way or format. This means that it can appear in lots of guises, some as simple as the phrases "Best before . . . ," "Better if used before . . . ," or "Sell by . . ."

Because durability indications can help avoid problems with food safety, it's thought that within the next few years a more prescriptive approach will be taken in this area, at least for items with the potential to do harm if not eaten within a specific period of time after production. This is especially important for goods such as yogurt and fresh meat, which spoil quite rapidly and could quickly become a danger to your health if not stored and used in the appropriate way.

For foods that aren't perishable (such as pasta, cookies, cereal, and canned drinks), this marking is less important from a food-safety point of view. But it's still desirable to have a clear indication of when to eat and how to store food in order to enjoy it at its best—and without any risk to your health. (Obviously, loose fruits and vegetables, as well as fresh breads and the like from bakeries, don't have durability indications and probably never will.)

Going Above and Beyond

In addition to the information that's required by law, there are other bits and pieces that can be included on labels, and it's up to each individual company whether or not to include them. Let's use the hypothetical spicy-tomato sauce that we talked about earlier in this chapter to explore the possibilities.

Remember that the makers of food and beverages usually create their labels with the goal of encouraging customers to reach up and put that product in their shopping cart, rather than a competitor's. So what further information might you put on your "Getting Saucy—The Spicy Tomato One" product to show it in the best possible light and persuade customers to buy it? Here are a few ideas:

- If it's especially low in fat, splash a "low fat" logo across the label. However, if you make any claim like this, then it must comply with specific laws defining the use of such expressions. (See Chapter 3 to find out more.)

- Tell customers if your sauce is suitable for vegetarians and whether it's organic.

- Volunteer (you aren't required to do so by law) that the food is free from certain substances that might trigger allergic reactions, such as wheat or eggs. This would be useful for someone following a special diet.

- Add information about exactly where the ingredients come from in order to make the product look appetizing and authentic, which might sway someone toward your particular brand.

- Proclaim special methods used in production (which you aren't required to disclose). Perhaps, for example, you oven-roasted the tomatoes to extract every last bit of flavor.

- To really go the extra mile, give more details about how to use the sauce, and maybe even provide a little recipe.

Keep in Mind . . .

Remember that labels are there to help you decide which food to buy. Knowing how to read the information allows you to discover what's really in different items, how they compare to similar products, and how they stand up in terms of quality and healthfulness.

Be aware that it's completely natural for manufacturers to make the most of any assets, and that they'll always tend to emphasize their good points while playing down their bad ones. If you want to make a comment or have a question, don't forget that you can always contact the company, whose details will be listed on the label.

With all the thousands of things that manufacturers are desperate to get you to put in your shopping basket, learning how to read labels will help you take control of what ends up in your cupboards, refrigerator, and freezer—and ultimately what you put into your body and what you feed your loved ones.

* * *

Chapter 2

Nutrition Labels

Flip over a box of food or turn a bottle around, and in almost every instance you'll find a bunch of figures telling you how much energy and how many nutrients the food or drink inside contains. This is known as the "nutrition facts" section of the label.

The legalities surrounding information that appears in this box are laid down by the Federal Food, Drug, and Cosmetics Act, which is a part of the Nutrition Labeling and Education Act that came into force in 1990.

That's the boring part—what you really need to know is that the laws make sure that what you read in the nutrition-facts box on bags, cartons, bottles, and cans is accurate, and presented in a consistent way between products as varied as breakfast cereals, baked beans, chips, and chocolate.

As you discovered in Chapter 1, meat and poultry have their own general laws that are controlled by the Food Safety Inspection Service, and the same is true here: They also have their own set of nutrition-labeling regulations.

The Nutrition-Facts Label Appearance

Unless the product is an odd shape and size, the preferred basic formatting for this information is very clearly defined. Manufacturers are given precise details regarding the typeface of each part of the label, including the letters, numbers, and lines drawn between the various sections.

That said, there are alternative tabular and linear versions that are also allowed for conveying the same information when packages are just too tricky in size and shape to opt for the basic version. Tabular displays are allowed where the vertical version just won't fit.

What's Included?

It's absolutely essential for manufacturers to provide the following details within their nutrition-facts label, with the information given per serving size:

- Total calories
- Calories from fat
- Total fat
- Saturated fat
- Trans fat
- Cholesterol
- Sodium
- Total carbohydrates

- Dietary fiber
- Sugars
- Protein
- Vitamin A
- Vitamin C
- Calcium
- Iron

The following information can be provided by manufacturers but is optional, unless they make a claim such as "rich in polyunsaturated fats" or "high in vitamin D," in which case the amount of the advertised component must be given.

- Calories from saturated fat
- Polyunsaturated fat
- Monounsaturated fat
- Potassium
- Soluble fiber
- Insoluble fiber
- Sugar alcohols (for example, xylitol, mannitol, or sorbitol)
- Other carbohydrates
- Other essential vitamins and minerals

No other nutrients may appear within the nutrition-facts section of the label (or "box"). If the manufacturer wants to give you more information—such as the amino-acid-protein building blocks present—then this would have to go outside of the official listing, somewhere else on the label's information panel.

The amounts are listed in grams (g), milligrams (mg), or micrograms (mcg) as appropriate, immediately to the right of the name. Manufacturers are allowed to give customers the number of calories provided per gram of fat (which is nine) and per gram of carbohydrate and protein (which is four).

Why List This Information?

The calories and nutrients that appear were chosen because they help people find out more information that relates to today's health concerns. The order in which they appear reflects the priority of current diet recommendations.

In practice, this means that you can see at a glance how many calories and how much total fat the product supplies per serving. This can then help you make sensible choices that control your weight and other factors, such as the risk of heart disease and diabetes.

Number of Servings

It's also necessary for the nutrition-facts label to provide the number of servings per package. This can be rounded to the nearest whole number (unless the servings are between 2 and 5, in which case the label can say, for example, 3.5), and servings must be given in familiar household measurements, along with the metric equivalent. It's optional, but you may also find a second set of numbers giving the nutrition information based on 100 g, 100 milliliters (ml), 1 ounce (oz), or 1 fluid ounce (fl oz) of the product. Be aware that a serving can be half a cookie, one muffin may actually contain three servings, and a bag of tortilla chips might have ten servings or more!

If the household measurement is a little vague, such as "a slice," then the weight or volume can be put in parentheses after the metric amount: "Serving size = 1 slice (28 g / 1 oz)."

% Daily Values

In addition to giving calories and amounts of nutrients and serving sizes, the nutrition-facts part of the label must also provide what's known as the "% Daily Value" of the nutrients.

These numbers are based on a 2,000-calorie daily diet and allow you to put the other information provided into context. If you just see an amount such as 150 mg of sodium, it may appear to be a lot, because 150 seems like a big number. In fact, this is only around 6 percent of the % Daily Value. Five grams of saturated fat, on the other hand, seems quite low, yet in reality is 25 percent of what you should be consuming each day.

Where the label is big enough to supply even more information within this section of the label, manufacturers are also allowed to say that in real life a person's individual-nutrient goals should be based on his or her particular calorie needs, since not everyone should actually consume 2,000 a day. Some people should eat more (such as male athletes), while others may need less (such as sedentary women). This advice is to help people understand that the % Daily Value is a guide, not a definitive statement of needs.

You're probably used to seeing all of the terms just described, but do you know what the word *calories* means, or what saturated fat actually is? And even if you do, how do you know how much is enough—and how much is too much? Let's take a closer look at the terms found in this section of food labels.

Calories

The energy a food gives your body is measured in kilocalories, which tends to be shortened to just "calories." You can't see them, and they aren't nutrients. They're just the way to measure the amount of energy present in a food, just as electrical energy is measured in watts. It's the carbohydrates, fat, protein, and alcohol in foods and beverages that actually contain calories, and therefore provide you with this power.

You need energy to run every single living process in your body. It fuels everything from the automatic beating of your heart to the deliberate use of your muscles when you walk, run, or jump. But if you consume too much energy from food and drinks, then the excess is just converted into fat, which means that you'll end up gaining weight.

If you wish to shed extra pounds, you need to take in fewer calories. A good place to start becoming aware of the energy content of different products is the nutrition-facts box on the label. And one of the first things most people look for is a food's fat content.

Fats

Strictly speaking, fats belong to a group of compounds that scientists call "lipids." When liquid at room temperature, they're known as oils (such as the olive oil used in salad dressings); when solid at room temperature, they're just referred to as fats (these include butter and margarine).

These ingredients are a very concentrated source of energy. Unlike protein and carbohydrates, they supply nine calories per gram. For example, the small amount of butter or margarine that you put on a piece of toast has at least 60 calories, while the much bigger slice of bread only has 70. The % Daily Value for fat (based on 2,000 calories per day) is less than 65 g.

For the purposes of the "total fat" figure in the nutrition-facts box, everything in this category is listed under the umbrella word "fat" and given in grams. "Calories from fat" is the amount of energy in the product that comes from ingredients such as butter, margarine, cream, or oils; and "calories from saturated fat" refers to the amount supplied specifically from that variety.

Saturated Fats

All fats are made up of building blocks known as "fatty acids," which come in three forms: saturated, monounsaturated, and polyunsaturated. You've probably seen these words many times on food labels in your kitchen.

Every fat—whether butter, margarine, or olive oil—is a mixture of all three types. What tends to happen, however, is that each food contains a different proportion of fatty acids. For example, butter is made up of 62 percent saturated, 30 percent mono-unsaturated, and 5 percent polyunsaturated fat. This means that it's a saturated fat, since that's the highest percentage. (See the table on page 61.)

The actual total grams that are specifically supplied by saturated fat are shown as "total saturated fat" in the nutrition-facts box. This substance is listed separately because it raises cholesterol in the blood, which may in turn increase the risk of heart disease. The % Daily Value for saturated fat (based on 2,000 calories a day) is less than 20 g.

Trans Fats

Trans fats occur naturally in some foods in very small amounts. However, they're created in larger quantities during the processing techniques used to make oils (naturally liquid at room temperature) into solid fats. They include vegetable shortenings and some margarines, which are used in foods such as crackers, cookies, and other snacks; fried foods; some salad dressings and baked goods; and many other processed foods.

Under new FDA regulations, by January 2006 these substances will have to be listed in the nutrition-facts box, just under the saturated figures. This information is being added because scientists have realized that trans fats raise LDL (bad cholesterol), which increases the risk of heart disease, and they lower HDL (good cholesterol), which is actually protective. Providing this information will allow shoppers to make more informed choices when it comes to cardiovascular health.

Poly- and Monounsaturated Fats

Listing the total amount of polyunsaturated fats is optional, but some manufacturers do include it. These fats tend to help lower LDL, so they're considered heart friendly.

Disclosing the quantity of monounsaturated fats is also optional. They're neutral when it comes to their effect on cholesterol levels in the blood, and they're also thought to be okay for your heart.

Cholesterol

Cholesterol levels in foods must be given in the nutrition-facts box. Most of the cholesterol in your blood is made in the liver from saturated fats. Some foods, however, contain it ready-made, including eggs, cheese, cream, and fatty pieces of meat.

The % Daily Value for cholesterol (based on 2,000 calories a day) is less than 300 mg.

Sodium

Sodium must also be listed in milligrams on this part of the food label. This trace mineral is present in very small amounts in substances such as the sodium bicarbonate in baking powder and the flavor enhancer monosodium glutamate (MSG). But these sources are tiny compared to the amounts eaten as sodium chloride—better known simply as salt.

The % Daily Value for sodium (based on 2,000 calories a day) is less than 2,300 mg or 2.3 g.

Potassium

Potassium is another trace mineral that's important in helping your body control fluid balance and blood pressure. Amounts (in milligrams) may be given, but it isn't mandatory.

Total Carbohydrates

The word *carbohydrate* means "carbon plus water." Carbs are basically compounds made by plants with access to water and exposure to rays of sunlight, and they come in starchy as well as sugary forms.

Starches are the main way in which plants store the energy that they need in order to grow and reproduce. These carbohydrates are long chains of sugars bonded together like the beads on a necklace. They're found in wheat and rice, and in foods made from these grains (such as bread, breakfast cereals, and rice cakes). Vegetables such as potatoes are also rich in starch.

Whether carbohydrates appear to be starchier or more sugary, they're all ultimately digested into their simplest form: glucose, which is the energy currency of every cell. This energy is provided at the rate of four calories per gram of carbohydrate (which is the same amount as protein).

Many types of carbohydrate foods also supply a range of other nutrients:

- An orange has 37 calories, most of which come from fruit sugar. It also provides practically your whole day's requirement of vitamin C.

- Bread's calories come from its starchy carbohydrates—77 calories in an average

slice—plus B vitamins naturally present in
the wheat from which the flour was made.

• Table sugar (sucrose), however, simply provides energy and contains no nutrients.

To get the total-carbohydrates figure in the nutrition-
facts box, all of these forms are added together and
given as one lump sum. No differentiation is made
between whether they come from starches or sugars. The Daily Value for total carbohydrate based on a
2,000-calorie-a-day diet is at least 300 g.

Further down the list of nutrients, carbs are broken down into separate figures for dietary fiber and
sugars.

Dietary Fiber

The health buzzword *fiber* refers to dietary fiber,
which is a kind of carbohydrate. It isn't found in animal products such as fish and meat, but rather in
plant foods (vegetables and fruits), and cereals such
as wheat and oats. The total amount of fiber in a food
is put on the nutrition label in grams. The Daily Value
for dietary fiber (based on 2,000 calories a day) is at
least 25 g.

There are two types of fiber: One is called "soluble" because when it's put in water, it forms a gel; sources include the pectin found in apples and pears. This substance helps slow down digestion and reduce cholesterol levels. The specific amount of soluble fiber can be listed separately in grams if the manufacturer chooses to do so.

The second type is referred to as "insoluble," and is found in places such as the fibrous husks of grains. This kind of fiber can't be broken down by human digestive systems. Unlike animals such as horses and sheep (which have special enzymes that dissolve the tough parts of plant material and then absorb them for energy), in humans this substance bulks up stools and passes out of the body undigested. This appears to reduce the risk of colon cancer and constipation. The specific amount of insoluble fiber can be listed separately in grams if a manufacturer wishes to do so.

Sugars

Sugars in food can be present naturally, such as the ones in fruit (fructose) and milk (lactose). But there are lots of added versions of sugars, too, which you may have seen on ingredients labels. They include:

- Sucrose
- Glucose
- Glucose syrup
- Golden syrup
- Maple syrup
- Fruit juices

- Invert sugar
- Honey
- Fructose
- Dextrose
- Maltose

The word *sugars* (which must be provided in the nutrition-facts box) could actually mean any of these, including naturally occurring fruit sugar (but it doesn't include lactose).

If you look at the nutrition information on a box of "100% shredded wheat" type of breakfast cereal, for example, you'll find that it contains no sugar. On the other hand, something like a frosted cereal can easily supply 20 g (five teaspoons) of sugar per 50 g serving.

Sugar Alcohols

These include sugar substitutes such as xylitol, sorbitol, and mannitol. They're types of sugar that are broken down and digested more slowly than sucrose, and that have fewer calories—approximately 2.5 calories instead of 4 calories per gram. In excess, they can cause gas and problems with bloating. Sugar alcohols don't have to be mentioned in the nutrition-facts box, but manufacturers can list them if they wish.

Other Carbohydrates

"Other carbohydrates" is another optional figure that may be given if the manufacturer chooses to do so. This is the difference between the total carbohydrates and the sum of total dietary fiber, sugars, and sugar alcohols.

Protein

Manufacturers must declare the amount of protein present in their products. Protein is an essential nutrient, and having a certain amount each day is crucial to your well-being. The word comes from the Greek *proteus* and means "of first quality."

Foods such as meat, chicken, turkey, fish, eggs, and milk; lentils, and soybean curd (tofu) all contain lots of protein, which is made up of chains of building blocks called "amino acids." Labels don't have to say exactly which amino acids are in a specific food or drink, but must only give the total amount of protein in grams. Once chewed, swallowed, and digested, this nutrient provides you not just with amino acids but also with energy.

Every gram of protein provides four calories. A very lean 6-oz steak contains 40 g (almost a whole day's supply) and has 327 calories, most of which come from this nutrient. The energy from the protein's amino acids is used to maintain and grow new cells throughout the body, from all those in muscles and skin to the cells that make hair and nails.

Vitamin A

Vitamin A levels must be declared. This nutrient is crucial for helping the membranes of your throat, nose, and eyes stay moist, and is also important for healthy reproductive and immune systems. It's fat soluble, which means that it's stored in your body (unlike vitamin C, which is water soluble and can be excreted in urine). Because it's not eliminated, it's possible to have too much vitamin A. This can cause problems for pregnant women, increasing the risk of birth defects in unborn children. All of these reasons show the importance of knowing the amount of vitamin A you're consuming.

In the nutrition-facts section of food and drink labels, vitamin A is expressed as a percent of the Daily Value, which is the amount you need to consume each day. The Daily Value for vitamin A is 5,000 International Units (IUs) a day.

Percent of Vitamin A as Beta-Carotene

Beta-carotene is a carotenoid, a natural orange pigment found in foods such as carrots and mangoes, as well as dark green vegetables such as spinach and broccoli (they look green instead of orange because the chlorophyll pigment is more dominant and covers the orange beta-carotene).

Your body can convert this nutrient into vitamin A. It isn't possible to overdose on beta-carotene because once your vitamin A stores are full, the conversion process stops. It's therefore considered a very safe way of meeting your needs for this nutrient. For this reason, some manufacturers also like to include the percentage of total vitamin A in their product that comes from beta-carotene, but this figure is optional.

Vitamin C

Listing the amount of vitamin C in a product is compulsory. This vitamin (scientific name: "ascorbic acid") is essential for making connective tissues in the body, such as the collagen under your skin, muscle tissue, and even bones.

This vital nutrient helps wounds heal and remain that way, and it's an important antioxidant, working to reduce potentially dangerous levels of free radicals that may otherwise trigger diseases such as cancer. It's also crucial for a healthy immune system. Amounts in food and drinks are, like vitamin A, expressed as a percent of the daily value, which is 75 mg a day for adults.

Calcium

Calcium content must also be provided in the nutrition-facts box. Around three pounds of your total body weight comes from calcium, which gives you an idea of just how important it is. While it's essential for strong bones and teeth—a widely known fact—it also plays vital roles in all kinds of other constant activities in the body, such as the contraction and relaxation of muscles, the regulation of fluid levels in cells, and even burning fat. Amounts of calcium are given as a percent of the daily value, which is 1,000 mg.

Iron

Iron is a mineral necessary for carrying oxygen in your blood. As such an important nutrient, it also must be declared on food labels. Insufficient iron causes fatigue and bad moods, and can even lead to hair loss. It also plays an important role in the production of many enzymes. It, too, is given as a percent of the daily value, which is 18 mg per day.

Other Vitamins and Minerals

Manufacturers aren't legally required to provide information about other vitamins or minerals unless they're mentioned elsewhere on the package. For example, if there's a claim somewhere on the product's information panel that the food is "high in vitamin E" or "fortified with vitamin B_1," then supporting details must be provided.

However, manufacturers aren't allowed to put

information about the levels of amino acids or the carbohydrate maltodextrin in the nutrition-facts section of the label. If they really want to mention these nutrients, then they must find space somewhere else on the package.

At-a-Glance Guide to Daily Values and % Daily Values (based on 2,000 Calories a Day)			
Nutrient	**Daily Value**	**% Daily Value**	**Goal***
Total fat	65 g	100%	Less than
Saturated fat	20 g	100%	Less than
Cholesterol	300 mg	100%	Less than
Sodium	2,400 mg	100%	Less than
Total carbohy-drate	300 g	100%	At least
Dietary fiber	25 g	100%	At least

What the Goal Means: This column refers to what you should strive for in your daily diet. Eating "less than" means just that: You should aim to consume less than the Daily Value (DV), which represents the maximum amount or upper limit of the nutrient that you should have each day. Eating "at least" also means just what it seems to. The standards for these categories, however, are in reverse: 25 g of fiber is the minimum recommended amount that you should get each day.

More on % Daily Values: A Quick Guide

When you see "5% DV" or less in a nutrition-facts box, you know that this number is low. This is good news if it describes nutrients that you're trying to cut down on, such as fat and saturated fat. If it applies to fiber—which you want to eat lots of—then you know that you'll need to eat other higher-fiber foods to reach your daily target.

A listing of "20% DV" or more is a high score, which is great if it applies to a vitamin or fiber. It's bad news if it appears next to nutrients you're trying to eat less of, such as fat and saturated fat.

In addition, these figures are useful in helping you look past a health claim such as "light" or "reduced fat" because you can cut to the chase and just compare the % Daily Value in each product. They also help you make dietary trade-offs: If you've eaten something that's giving you more than 20% of the Daily Value of fat, then you can trade it off against low-fat foods later in the day.

Nutrients Without % Daily Values

The following substances may often appear in the nutrition-facts box without Daily Values:

- **Trans fats:** Experts haven't yet been able to provide concrete guidelines for the consumption of trans fats. The general advice is to choose as few products as possible containing them.

- **Protein:** If a claim such as "high in protein" is made on the packaging, then a % Daily Value must be provided. Otherwise, it may be omitted.

- **Sugars:** There's no % Daily Value for this nutrient. To limit your intake of added sugars, check the ingredients list and avoid products that contain any of the various forms mentioned earlier in this chapter.

At-a-Glance Recommended Daily Allowances		
Each Day	**Women**	**Men**
Total calories	2,000	2,500
Calories from fat	30% or less	30% or less
Total fat	65 g	80 g
Saturated fat	20 g	25 g
Cholesterol	less than 300 mg	less than 300 mg
Sodium	2.3 mg	2.3 mg
Total carbohydrate	300 g	375 g
Dietary fiber	25 g	38 g
Sugars	10% of total calories	10% of total calories
Vitamin A	700 micrograms (mcg)	90 micrograms (mcg)
Vitamin C	75 mg	90 mg
Calcium	1,000 mg (ages 19–50)	1,000 mg (ages 19–50)
	1,200 mg (age 50+)	1,200 mg (age 50+)
Iron	18 mg (ages 19–50)	8 mg
	8 mg (age 50+)	

Why Does It Matter?

Maybe you're wondering what all the fuss is about over nutrients. So what if you eat a lot of sugar, not much fiber, or have more than the daily value of fat? What's the problem with too much of this or too little of that? In fact, there are definite consequences to each one of these behaviors.

Too Much Fat

Just one tablespoon (15 g) of fat such as butter or margarine provides 111 calories worth of energy once digested and absorbed. Because it's such a concentrated source of energy, it's easy to go overboard and rack up the calories when putting away foods and beverages (such as many coffee drinks) that are rich in fat. And excess calories lead to weight gain, which is associated with many health problems such as diabetes and high blood pressure.

Too Much Saturated Fat

After eating products containing saturated fats, the blood levels of bad cholesterol (LDL) go up. Raised LDL increases the risk of cholesterol sticking to blood-vessel walls and causing blockages, which can trigger a heart attack or stroke.

But eating polyunsaturated fats (such as those

found in sunflower oil, nuts, and seeds) seems to help lower the amount of LDL in the blood slightly. Monounsaturated fats (such as those in olive oil), on the other hand, tend to have a neutral effect on bad cholesterol.

At-a-Glance Guide to Types of Fat				
Type of fat	**% Satu- rated Fat**	**% Mono- unsat. Fat**	**% Poly- unsat. Fat**	**Known As**
Olive oil	14	74	9	Monounsaturated
Rapeseed oil	8	59	32	Monounsaturated
Sunflower oil	12	22	66	Polyunsaturated
Soybean oil	9	23	51	Polyunsaturated
Butter	62	30	5	Saturated
Palm oil	47	44	9	Saturated

Too Little Fiber

As I mentioned earlier, fiber comes in two forms. One type—found in items such as apples, pears, and oats—is known as soluble fiber. When you eat foods rich in this nutrient, the gel that forms in your digestive system has the benefit of making you feel full, and it also seems to help lower the cholesterol circulating in your blood.

The other type, insoluble fiber, is found in foods such as whole-grain bread and breakfast cereals and brown rice. This husky, fibrous substance that you can't break down moves through your upper intestine and into your colon. Because it absorbs water, it bulks up your stools so that they pass through easily. By speeding movement through the colon, it also seems to help remove potential toxins and carcinogens. Not having enough insoluble fiber may increase the risk of bowel problems such as constipation, and even cancer.

Adults in the U.S. eat around 15 g of fiber a day, much less than the target of 25 g of total fiber, which means that most people need to increase their consumption of vegetables, fruit, and whole-grain foods in order to gain these health benefits and follow a balanced diet.

Too Much Sodium or Salt

At the moment, we're packing away around 15 g of salt a day—that is, 6 g of sodium. It's recommended that adults don't actually have more than 6 g a day (2.3 g sodium). Children's intake should be graded according to their age (see Chapter 7 for more information).

In most people, high salt intake raises blood pressure, which in turn increases the likelihood of having a heart attack or stroke. A salt-rich diet has been linked to an increased risk of developing the bone-thinning disease osteoporosis, and it also tends to encourage your body to hang on to excess fluids. By reducing this mineral to less than 3 g a day (1.2 g sodium), it's been suggested that you could lose one and a half liters of fluid—which amounts to three pounds of body weight!

Too Much Sugar

As you've seen, sugar comes in many forms. None of these supply anything other than energy, which means that they are, in nutrition-speak, "empty calories." In other words, when added to foods and drinks, they don't bring any useful vitamins or minerals with them, just energy. Therefore, the general advice is to keep them as low as possible. What's the point in wasting calories that could be packing in the precious nutrients you need each day to keep looking and feeling your best?

And having sugary foods and beverages between meals, at times when you can't brush your teeth, provides an ideal environment in your mouth for the growth of decay-causing bacteria. Steering away from such snacks and drinks between meals is a good idea if you want to keep cavities and gum disease at bay.

Keep in Mind . . .

Research shows that labels can help provide education in the supermarket, so they're definitely worth reading! Remember that the nutrition-facts box should help you understand what contribution a food or drink is making to your diet, and that the manufacturer is obliged by law to supply this information.

Using the % Daily Values when you're out shopping can help you interpret the meaning of the nutrient information. Just keep in mind that these percentages are based on a diet of 2,000 calories a day. The numbers are only intended to be a guide: Some individuals need more than what's specified and some need less.

In addition, always check the ingredients as well as the nutrition-facts box; it will help you understand what's in the product. If you use that list together with the information in this chapter, you can get to the bottom of nutrition labeling. It will help you make sense of, and put into perspective, the next chapter on nutrition claims, ensuring that you understand them for what they are.

* * *

Chapter 3

Nutrition Claims

"Low fat," "high fiber," and "reduced sugar"—it's so common for these kinds of things to be splashed across food labels nowadays that it's hard to imagine that even just 25 years ago they were almost unheard of.

Most people know which foods are naturally low in fat (vegetables and fruit, for example) and which are high in fiber (whole-grain bread). However, these days there are so many processed foods and drinks on the shelves that at first glance it can be hard to figure out which category many of them fit into. So it's left to manufacturers to tell us—and boy do they love it! How often have you seen products with logos saying that a food is "low in salt" or "sugar-free"? You probably also encounter lots of labels with descriptions such as "reduced fat," "more fiber," "only 200 mg of sodium," and "lite." When you understand what they mean, these words may help you decide what to put in your shopping basket.

This issue is regulated under the Nutrition Labeling and Education Act of 1990, which gives very clear instructions so that the descriptions used are consistent across all products. Claims can only be made for nutrients that have Daily Values, and this chapter catalogs the specific criteria for each term.

Common Label Terms

It may seem pretty clear that when a label says a product is "lean" or "low in sodium," that it actually is, but again, we must read closer for accuracy. Following are the most common nutrition claims on labels, along with what each *really* means.

"Free"

This means that the product contains none—or only tiny amounts of—the nutrient listed, which will therefore have virtually no effect on your body. It can apply to fat, saturated fat, cholesterol, sodium, sugars, and calories:

- Calorie-free: less than 5 calories per serving
- Sugar-free: less than 0.5 g of sugar per serving
- Fat-free: less than 0.5 g of fat per serving

Manufacturers can also use certain other words in place of free:

- Without
- No
- Zero
- Skim (most often used with dairy products)

"Low"

The word *low* can be used to describe fat, saturated fat, cholesterol, sodium, and calories. It means that the food or drink can be consumed quite frequently if you're following healthy-eating dietary guidelines. Here are some common terms and the levels of these nutrients that the product must contain in order to make the claim:

- Low calorie: 40 calories or less per serving
- Low fat: less than 3 g per serving
- Low saturated fat: 1 g or less per serving

- Low sodium: 140 mg or less per serving
- Low cholesterol: less than 20 mg of cholesterol, or 2 g or less of saturated fat per serving

Manufacturers can also use certain other words that have the same meaning as "low," with the same criteria:

- Little
- Few
- Low source of
- Contains a small amount of

"Lean and Extra Lean"

You'll see the words *lean* and *extra lean* on products containing meat, fish, poultry, and game meats (such as venison). In order to say that something is lean, manufacturers must make sure that the product meets these criteria per serving and per 100 g:

- Less than 10 g of fat
- 4.5 g or less of saturated fat
- Less than 95 mg of cholesterol

To describe a product as "extra lean," the manufacturer must be able to prove that it contains these amounts per serving and per 100 g:

- Less than 5 g of fat
- Less than 2 g of saturated fat
- Less than 95 mg of cholesterol

The exception to these rules is the labeling of ground beef.

"High," "Rich in," or "Excellent Source of"

These are all emotionally charged words that can really sway the decision-making process, so it's definitely worth figuring out what they actually mean. The fact is that a manufacturer can only use these terms if they can prove that their product contains 20 percent or more of the Daily Value of the featured nutrient in a typical serving.

For example, the Daily Value for vitamin C is 60 mg. If a serving of freshly squeezed orange juice supplies 15 mg of vitamin C, then it would qualify for special attention on the nutrition label in one of the following forms:

- High in vitamin C
- Rich in vitamin C
- An excellent source of vitamin C

"High Potency"

You'll probably agree that "high potency" is an even more powerful nutrition claim than the previous terms. It really pushes the idea that this product is packed with certain vitamins or minerals. The legal definition states that a product contains 100 percent or more of the Daily Value of the nutrients mentioned. On a multi-ingredient food, this term can be used if the product contains more than 100 percent of the daily value of at least two-thirds of the vitamins and minerals that have Daily Values.

In reality, you'll usually see this description on multivitamin and mineral supplements rather than regular foods and beverages.

"Good Source of," "Contains," or "Provides"

These are much more common nutrition claims that you'll see on many boxes and cans. If you pick up a product with one of these terms, then the food or drink inside should have 10 to 19 percent of the Daily Value of the nutrient mentioned. For example, a type of yogurt may claim to be "a good source of calcium." If it does, then it means that a typical serving supplies at least 100 mg of calcium, which is needed to build and maintain strong bones.

"Reduced"

Here's another common word that you'll see on products scattered around supermarket shelves. To be used, the manufacturer must be sure that this version of the product contains at least 25 percent less of the specified nutrient or calories than the regular item. For instance, reduced-fat guacamole can be labeled as such if it has 12 g of fat per 100 g, compared to a standard version that contains 16 g of fat per 100 g.

This word can't be used if the food or drink is already labeled "low" (or one of its equivalents).

"Less"

Whether or not a food has been nutritionally altered, it can bear the word *less* if it contains 25 percent less of a nutrient or calories than the referenced standard product. For example, pretzels that have 25 percent less fat than potato chips could use this claim.

The term *fewer* is interchangeable with *less.*

"Light"

Here's a case where it's easy to make mistakes: On the one hand, this can be used to describe nutritional content; and on the other, it can refer to the texture or color of food (such as light-brown sugar).

When "light" applies to nutritional content, it means that the product has been altered in such a way as to lower the calories by one-third, or that it has half the fat of the standard reference food. Generally, a percentage reduction for both the fat and calories must be provided, although if the food is already a low-fat version, then manufacturers don't need to supply this extra information. The term can also be applied to sodium when that nutrient has been slashed by half.

If the reference food originally had more than half of its calories coming from fat (such as a rich cheesecake), then the reduction in fat must be by 50 percent to qualify for the "light" nutritional claim.

You can see that just because a label uses this word doesn't mean that it's necessarily good for you. A product can have 33 percent fewer calories than the original food, but the final light version may still be pretty high in total calories.

"More," "Added," "Extra," or "Plus"

These claims can be used on standard or nutritionally altered foods and drinks that supply at least 10 percent of the Daily Value of the nutrient referred to.

The words *fortified* and *enriched* can also be used when the product provides 10 percent or more of the Daily Value of the nutrient, although they can only be put on items that have in some way already been nutritionally altered (such as a fruit drink with reduced sugar). It's also useful to be aware that these expressions are interchangeable with the word *hi,* and the word *lo* may be used to indicate reduced ingredients, such as sugar.

"Modified"

You may also have seen the word *modified* on food packaging. This can be used as long as it's followed by an explanation of the modification. Such a label might read: "Modified-fat cheesecake—contains 35 percent less fat than our regular cheesecake."

The best strategy when you see this—or any other nutrition claim, for that matter—is to check out the nutrition-facts section of the label and figure out exactly how many total calories and how much total fat you're getting per serving.

"Healthy"

It used to be that when someone said, "Oh, that's healthy," they were probably referring to an apple or another piece of fruit. Nowadays, for a manufacturer to claim that their product is healthy, they have to prove that it meets standard criteria. A healthy food must be low in fat and saturated fat and contain limited amounts of cholesterol and sodium. (In single foods, the sodium must not be more than 360 mg per serving, and not more than 480 mg per serving in whole-meal products.)

Raw, frozen, and canned fruits and vegetables that haven't been nutritionally altered due to the processing are exempt from this rule and can be labeled "healthy" anyway. Other foods, such as frozen entrées and multicourse frozen dinners, must supply 10 percent of two or three vitamins, minerals, protein, or fiber to be able to carry this label, in addition to meeting the criteria of also being low in fat and so on.

"Fiber"

While it's okay to say that a food is high in fiber, if the product's fat content is more than 3 g per 100 g, then the total fat per serving must be clearly marked. This helps you avoid automatically thinking, *Oh, it's high in fiber, so it must be good for me.* Some cookies are a good case in point: They may have enough fiber to qualify for a high-fiber claim, but if they also have a lot of fat, then at least you'll know about it.

"% Fat-Free"

A product label can only carry the claim that it's x% fat free if it's low in fat to begin with (in other words, has less than 3 g per serving) or is fat-free (less than 0.5 g per serving). For example, if a frozen spaghetti dinner has only 9 g of fat per 300 g serving, it can claim to be "97% fat-free."

"Sugar"

The terms *no added sugar* and *without added sugar* can be used on labels if no sugar or sugar-containing ingredients (such as maple syrup) are added during the processing of the food. "Unsweetened" and "no added sweeteners," on the other hand, aren't considered nutritional claims, but simply statements of fact.

"Antioxidants"

A claim that a food or drink contains antioxidants can be put on the label if a Daily Value exists for this nutrient, and it's been scientifically proven to have antioxidant activity. It can only be mentioned, how-ever, if the amount in the food or drink gives you enough to meet the requirements for making a high, good-source, or high-potency claim. Orange juice with added vitamins C and E is a good candidate for this term.

Implied Claims

Manufacturers may try to get away with imply-ing that their products are better for you than they really are, but they have to watch out, because doing so is illegal. For example, a company might want to create a special graphic stating that a cereal bar is made with oat bran, which implies that it will be rich in fiber. But if the end product doesn't actually pro-vide enough fiber to be considered a good source of the nutrient (10 to 19 percent of the Daily Value or 2.5 to 4.75 g of total fiber), then this reference isn't allowed. If, on the other hand, the amount of oat bran does meet this requirement, then it's fine.

Some similar statements, however, are permitted and don't count as implied claims:

- A product can claim to be 100 percent milk-free if it's in the context of telling people that the food is suitable for those avoiding milk and milk products due to a food intolerance or for religious reasons.

- It's also okay for the manufacturer to tell customers that an item is free from non-nutritive substances such as artificial colors.

An exception to the implied claim regulations is what's known as an "equivalence" claim, when the food to which the item is being compared is a good source of the nutrient in question. For example, a manufacturer could make an equivalence claim for an orange drink by stating on the bottle: "Contains as much vitamin C as an 8-oz glass of orange juice."

Frequently Asked Questions

Q. Why do some brands of reduced-fat chips contain more fat than standard versions of other chips?

A. The term *reduced fat* applies to the reduction compared to the same brand's full-fat version. If brand X has quite a bit more fat than brand Y, then brand

X's reduced-fat version may still have more total fat than brand Y's original version. Always check the per-total-serving information in the label's nutrition-facts box if you're consciously cutting down on fat.

Q. If a food claims to be low fat, can I assume that it's good for me?

A. Not necessarily. For example, it could be low in fat yet high in sugar. Low-fat and reduced-fat cakes and cookies are a classic example of this kind of pitfall, because when manufacturers lower the amount of fat in a recipe, they have to put something else in to replace it, otherwise there won't be sufficient bulk. Usually, when fat is cut, sugar is piled in to take its place. So you might pat yourself on the back for choosing a low-fat cookie while unwittingly wading into a food that's jam-packed with sugar.

In the long run, this can be a problem if you're watching your weight, because sometimes the massive amounts of sugar added to replace the fat bring the final calories up to pretty much the same as those in the original version—crazy, but true!

Q. Then how can I make sense of low-fat claims?

A. Don't rely on that statement. Instead, take a look at how many calories you're getting per serving of the food. If you're watching your weight, then at the end of the day, it's the total number of calories you're eating that will make the difference on the scale.

Q. I always think, *Oh great, because this food is low in fat, or reduced in fat, then I might as well have two!* I guess that isn't very smart, is it?

A. It's another little trap, and it's only human nature to fall into it. The idea that you're being good because you're selecting a low-fat food can make it really tempting to eat more. But if you do this, you'd probably have been better off just having one helping of the standard version of the product.

Q. Many of the things I see in the supermarkets say that they have added calcium or minerals. Are these good ways to get extra nutrients? For example, is the calcium added to some orange juice as good as getting it from milk or other dairy products?

A. Some items, such as orange juice or soy milk, can be really useful sources of this particular nutrient, especially for people who don't eat dairy. However, I've seen "added calcium" splashed across processed-cheese foods being marketed for children's lunch boxes. These products are rich in salt, contain quite a lot of additives, and have questionable overall-nutritional value. In such cases, the calcium claim is a bit misleading in terms of how healthy the item is.

Keep in Mind . . .

Always remember:

- Don't be seduced by first impressions.

- Don't take every claim you see at face value.

- Flip the product over and take a look at the nutrient-facts section of the label so that you know what you're really eating per serving.

- Only add it to your cart when you're completely satisfied that a product is what it seems.

- If in doubt, leave it on the shelf.

In the next chapter, we'll look at yet another set of claims, which asserts how foods can help you avoid certain diseases and physical conditions.

* * *

Chapter 4

Health Claims

The idea that certain foods and drinks are good for you isn't new. You've probably heard that fish benefits your brain and that carrots help you see in the dark—this knowledge has been passed down over the centuries. The interesting thing is that scientists today, even with all of their high-tech equipment and research tools, are proving that much of this folklore is true.

In spite of "just knowing" that some things are particularly great for health, prior to 1993 it was illegal to make any assertions on packages and labels that a food or drink might have health benefits. After much deliberation, the Food and Drug Administration decided that specific claims could be made if—and only if—very sound scientific studies proved that they're valid. Old wives' tales weren't enough for the FDA to approve something! Of course this is a good thing, because if the situation wasn't tightly controlled, it could easily be abused.

The good news these days is that there's quite a wide variety of health claims that can appear on an assortment of goods, helping you make good decisions when you shop.

How Health Claims Can Appear

These statements can be made in several ways:

- Via a third party, such as the National Cancer Institute.

- Through the use of symbols such as the American Heart Association's red heart with a white check mark.

- With a written description on the label.

Whichever method is chosen, it isn't possible for a manufacturer to make any statement at all unless it's authorized by the FDA, which allows two types of health claims. The first are "general and approved health claims," of which there are currently 12 in total. These can only be made when the FDA states that there's significant agreement or overwhelming and indisputable scientific work confirming the link between eating certain foods and nutrients and their potential role in reducing the risk of disease.

The second are "qualified health claims," which are interim-type measurements for when there's a certain level of scientific evidence linking a food or nutrient to reducing the risk of disease, but it hasn't yet been completely proven.

Let's now take a closer look at these two very different types of health claims.

General and Approved Health Claims

Even when a claim has been authorized, it can only provide information about the food or drink's ability to play a role in possibly reducing the risk of developing a disease. The words *may* or *might* must be used, and to be sure that no one is misled into thinking that their diet is the only cause of the disease, the food manufacturer must also say that other factors play a role.

A good example is the claim allowed on poly-unsaturated, low-cholesterol spreads (such as some butter substitutes) which can state on their labels: "While many factors affect heart disease, diets low in saturated fat and cholesterol may reduce the risk of this disease."

No health claim can be made on a food or drink that has a certain benefit, on the one hand, such as being low in cholesterol, if on the other it's high in total fat. To ensure compliance with this rule, products must meet these criteria (per serving size) in order to qualify for a health claim of any type:

- No more than 13 g of total fat
- No more than 4 g of saturated fat
- No more than 60 mg of cholesterol
- No more than 480 mg of sodium

These limits have been set for single items, such as a serving of breakfast cereal or a glass of juice. For products designed to be eaten as an entire main dish, such as a frozen meal of cannelloni, the amounts are slightly higher:

- No more than 26 g of total fat
- No more than 8 g of saturated fat
- No more than 120 mg of cholesterol
- No more than 960 mg of sodium

In addition to meeting these criteria, a health claim can't be made unless the food or drink contains

10 percent or more of the Daily Value for at least one of the following nutrients, without being fortified (that is, having them added):

- Vitamin A: 500 IU
- Vitamin C: 6 mg
- Iron: 1.8 mg
- Calcium: 100 mg
- Protein: 5 g
- Fiber: 2.5 g

It's also very important that the statement is complete, truthful, not misleading, and enables you to understand both the facts provided and the significance of that data within the context of your total daily diet. All of the relevant information must appear in the same spot on the label and packaging—not scattered all over the place.

Let's take a look at the details of the approved health claims—the type of wording that manufacturers can use, and examples of foods and drinks on which they can appear.

Calcium and Osteoporosis

Osteoporosis is a serious disease in which bones lose their strength and become prone to fractures. Apart from the obvious pain associated with breaking a wrist or hip, this condition causes disability, immobility, and even a hunchback appearance when the spine curves due to damaged vertebrae. Because the lungs and digestive system get "crunched up" through the permanent stooping this causes, breathing can become labored, and indigestion may be an uncomfortable part of everyday life.

Anything that can help reduce the incidence of osteoporosis is crucial. Besides ensuring that you eat enough of the bone-building mineral calcium, which plays a part in fighting this disease, the FDA has allowed manufacturers to use certain claims on foods and drinks if they're rich in this mineral. These statements are especially aimed at the groups of people who may not consume sufficient amounts in their diets. Here's an example of what you may see on items such as milk and yogurt: "Regular exercise and a healthy diet with enough calcium help teens and young adult white and Asian women maintain good bone health and may reduce their high risk of osteoporosis later in life."

To carry this claim, a food must contain 20 percent or more of the Daily Value for calcium—that is, at least 200 mg in a typical serving—but that's not all. The mineral must be in a form that the body finds easy to absorb. The product must also have at least the same amount of another mineral called phosphorus, because calcium works best when it's present.

If the item is especially high in calcium and contains, for instance, 40 percent or more of the Daily Value, then the label must make it clear that having more than 2,000 mg a day has no known extra benefit. This is to help stop you from mistakenly thinking that you can't get too much of a good thing. The fact is that ingesting sufficient calcium helps improve your chance of building and maintaining strong bones and may reduce the risk of osteoporosis. Taking in a lot more doesn't have any added benefit and could actually put your body under stress from having to dispose of the excess quantities.

Dietary Fat and Cancer

The World Cancer Research Fund and the American Institute for Cancer Research have both reached the conclusion that if you eat a lot of fat, it may increase the risk of certain cancers developing, particularly those of the lungs, colon, rectum, breast, and prostate. The FDA allows manufacturers to point out this potential link on their products with a health claim along these lines: "Development of cancer depends on many factors. A diet low in total fat may reduce the risk of some cancers."

To carry this notice, the food must meet the nutrient-content-claim requirements for being low fat: 3 g or less of total fat per serving. For fish and meat to make such a claim, they must be extra lean: less than 5 g of fat, less than 2 g of saturated fat, and less than 95 mg of cholesterol per serving and per 100 g.

Dietary Saturated Fat and Cholesterol and Coronary Heart Disease (CHD)

The World Cancer Research Fund and American Institute for Cancer Research also reached the conclusion that eating a lot of saturated and animal fats may increase the risk of lung, colon, rectum, breast, endometrium, and prostate cancer. A health claim drawing attention to this can therefore be made on certain products. For example, you may see the following kind of statement: "While many factors affect

heart disease, diets low in saturated fat and cholesterol may reduce the risk of this disease."

The FDA will allow manufacturers to mention this
potential link between reduced risk of CHD and lower
saturated fat and cholesterol intakes if they meet certain criteria:

- Low fat: 3 g or less fat per serving

- Low saturated fat: 1 g or less saturated fat
  per serving

- Low cholesterol: 20 mg or less cholesterol
  per serving

- Fish and meat must be extra lean: less than
  5 g of fat per serving

- If, within the health claim, the manufacturer
  makes any specific reference to definitions
  of what constitutes "high" or "normal" cholesterol levels, then they must also include
  a "physician statement" saying that people
  with elevated LDL or total cholesterol should
  consult their doctors.

Fruits, Vegetables,
and Grain Products . . . and Cancer

Experts who have looked at all the evidence from scientific studies around the world have concluded that when diets have a good supply of whole-grain fiber (such as that found in some bread and pasta), fruits, and vegetables, there may be a reduced risk of developing cancer. Links have especially been made between a good intake of whole-grain cereals and reducing the potential for stomach cancer; and high consumption of fruits and vegetables and decreasing the risk of mouth, larynx, pharynx, esophagus, lung, pancreas, breast, stomach, and bladder cancer. Vegetables seem to be particularly helpful in lowering the possibility of cancer of the colon and rectum.

Because of this evidence, it's acceptable for manufacturers to make certain claims drawing your attention to these links. You might see something like this: "Low-fat diets rich in fiber-containing grain products, fruits, and vegetables may reduce the risk of some types of cancer, a disease associated with many factors." The product doesn't need to describe exactly which type of fiber it's supplying, which may be soluble, insoluble, or a mix of both.

To make this claim, a food such as multigrain

flour, bread, or breakfast cereal must supply 10 to 19 percent of the Daily Value of fiber, which is 2.5 to 4.75 g of fiber per serving, and must also be low fat. Items fortified with fiber aren't allowed to use this statement.

The same rules apply for fruits and vegetables, and in both cases, the nutrient must be naturally present. In addition, the FDA permits manufacturers to make a statement similar to the one just described, but with the addition of a phrase specifying that vitamin A and vitamin C may be beneficial. This claim may be used for fruit and vegetable products that meet the nutrient-content-claim requirements for being low fat and are a good source of at least one of the specified vitamins, without fortification (10 to 19 percent of the Daily Values: 500 to 950 IU for vitamin A and 6 to 11.4 mg for vitamin C).

Fruits, Vegetables, and Grain Products . . . and CHD

There's also a scientifically proven link between eating plenty of fruits, vegetables, and fiber-rich grains and a lower chance of developing coronary heart disease. This is probably because such foods are rich in a huge range of protective antioxidants that are thought to help reduce the chances of your arteries becoming clogged with cholesterol. Because of this, manufacturers are able to make a statement such as: "Diets low in saturated fat and cholesterol and rich in fruits, vegetables, and grain products that contain some types of dietary fiber, particularly soluble fiber, may reduce the risk of heart disease, a disease associated with many factors."

To make this claim, a food must be (or contain) fruits, vegetables, and grain products. It also has to meet the nutrient-content-claim requirements for low saturated fat, low cholesterol, and low fat; and contain, without fortification, at least 0.6 g soluble fiber per serving.

If the manufacturer makes any specific reference to definitions of what constitutes high or normal cholesterol levels within the health claim, then the product must also include the physician statement described in the preceding section.

Sodium and Hypertension (High Blood Pressure)

There's good scientific research indicating that increases in blood pressure can be caused by eating a lot of sodium (salt), and that this leads to an increased chance of developing heart disease and a higher probability of having a stroke. For this reason, it's good to be aware if foods are especially low in sodium. Those that are may carry this kind of statement: "Diets low in sodium may reduce the risk of high blood pressure, a disease associated with many factors."

To make this claim, a food must meet the nutrient-content-claim requirements for low sodium, which means that it must have 140 mg or less of sodium per serving. If any mention is made on the package that gives a definition of high or normal blood pressure, then it must also provide a physician statement, advising people with high blood pressure to consult their doctor.

Folic Acid and Neural-Tube Defects

As a baby is growing in the womb, one of the first parts of its body to develop is something called the "neural tube." It starts off as a plate of nerve cells that rolls over onto itself to create a tube, and then goes on to develop into the spine. The process happens very early on in pregnancy, around 20 to 28 days after conception. If the nerve material doesn't fuse all the way down, then a neural-tube defect occurs. When this failure occurs at the bottom of the spine, the condition is known as spina bifida.

It's been shown that levels in a woman's blood of the B vitamin called folate somehow affect this development. Diets rich in this nutrient appear to encourage closure of the tube and may reduce the risk of a child being born with one or more of these defects.

The trouble is that the formation of the spine occurs so early on that most women don't even know they're pregnant when it's happening, and once they do know (say at five weeks), eating more folate is pointless. For this reason, it's important that all women of childbearing age, who may intentionally or unintentionally become pregnant, eat diets rich in folate.

The FDA allows claims on the labels of foods with high quantities of this nutrient, such as: "Healthful diets with adequate folate may reduce a woman's risk of having a child with a brain or spinal defect." It may also refer to other forms of the nutrient, which include folic acid and folacin, and it must alert consumers that the defects may have many causes. The label also has to give the safe maximum daily limit for this B vitamin.

This kind of claim is allowed on dietary supplements and foods. They must contain sufficient folate, but not provide more than 100 percent of the Daily Value for vitamin A as retinol, preformed vitamin A, or vitamin D, since too much of these fat-soluble vitamins may be harmful to a pregnant woman and her developing baby.

Dietary Sugar Alcohols and Dental Caries (Cavities)

Many of us have been told since childhood not to eat too many sweets and sugary foods, since doing so will lead to rotten teeth. It seems that everyone who said this was right! There's a link between having sugary foods and drinks between mealtimes and an increased chance of developing tooth decay. Certain claims can therefore be made for foods that will *not* have this effect.

The products that take advantage of this tend to be sugar-free candies and chewing gums, which use alternative sweeteners that are known not to promote tooth decay. The claims they're allowed to make include statements like this: "Frequent between-meal consumption of foods high in sugars and starches promotes tooth decay. The sugar alcohols [names of those used must be provided] do not promote tooth decay." The sugar alcohols you may see listed include:

- Xylitol
- Sorbitol
- Mannitol
- Maltitol
- Isomalt
- Lactitol
- Hydrogenated starch hydrolysates
- Hydrogenated glucose syrups

As with many health claims, this is quite a bit of text and takes up a lot of room. For products with limited space, such as packs of gum with less than 15 square inches of space, it's acceptable to use a simpler claim, such as: "Does not promote tooth decay." Labels carrying this type of information must also say that frequently eating foods high in sugars and starches between meals promotes tooth decay.

Soluble Fiber and Heart Disease

There's evidence that eating foods rich in soluble fiber (the type that forms a gel in your stomach and intestines) helps lower cholesterol levels in your blood, and therefore helps lower your chance of developing heart disease. For this reason, certain claims may be made to draw your attention to especially good suppliers of this nutrient. The package might say: "Soluble fiber from foods such as [mention the type of food] as part of a diet low in saturated fat and cholesterol may reduce the risk of heart disease. A serving of [mention the type of food again] supplies x grams [give the weight] of soluble fiber [give its name] necessary per day to have this effect."

To be able to make this claim, the food must contain a source of whole oats or psyllium-seed husks and must provide:

- Beta-glucan from oat bran with at least 5.5% beta-glucan
- Beta-glucan from rolled oats or oatmeal with at least 4% beta-glucan
- Beta-glucan from whole-oat flour with at least 4% beta-glucan
- Beta-glucan-soluble fiber or psyllium husk with purity of no less than 95%

In addition, the product must be:

- Low in saturated fat
- Low in fat
- Low in cholesterol

Because the item is making a health claim for soluble fiber, the amount of that nutrient in a serving of the food must be listed on the nutrition-facts panel of the label.

A product supplying soluble fiber from psyllium must also make the point that it needs to be consumed with adequate quantities of water, because the husks swell up quickly when in contact with saliva and may cause choking if taken without fluids. A warning such as this may be used: "This food should be eaten with at least a full glass of liquid. Eating this product without enough liquid may cause choking. Do not eat this product if you have difficulty swallowing."

Plant Sterol/Stanol Esters and CHD

Plant sterol and stanol esters may sound like complex, human-made chemicals, but they do exist naturally in some plants. Research has discovered that they play a role in helping lower blood levels of LDL or "bad" cholesterol by latching on to it in the digestive system and carrying it out of the body in stools. This helps protect against the ravages of heart disease.

Scientists are able to produce these potentially protective plant derivatives and add them to certain foods such as yogurt, salad dressing, and butter-type spreads. These kinds of foods can therefore carry certain health claims such as: "Foods containing at least 0.65 g per serving of vegetable oil sterol esters, eaten twice a day with meals for a daily total intake of at least 1.3 g, as part of a diet low in saturated fat and cholesterol, may reduce the risk of heart disease. A serving of [name of the food] supplies X g of vegetable oil sterol esters."

The item must be low in saturated fat and cholesterol to be eligible for this health claim. Because foods such as spreads and salad dressing are implicitly high in fat, those with more than 13 g of fat per 50 g must also state: "See nutrition information for fat content." This is to help keep you from thinking that you can eat as much as you want!

Soy Protein and CHD

Scientists have also made a link between eating the special type of protein present in soy and foods containing soy and a reduction in levels of bad cholesterol, which lowers the chances of developing heart disease. The FDA has therefore made it possible for manufacturers to make the following kinds of claims on foods rich in this substance: "25 g of soy protein a day, as part of a diet low in saturated fat and cholesterol, may reduce the risk of heart disease. A serving of [name of the food] supplies X g of soy protein."

In order for soy-based foods or drinks to carry this kind of health claim, they must also be low in saturated fat, total fat, and cholesterol. However, an exception to this rule is food made from whole soybeans, which naturally supply 7 g of fat per 100 g (to qualify as low fat, a food needs to have 3 g or less per serving). But if a product is made from whole soybeans and has extra fat *added* (such as soy burgers), then it wouldn't be allowed to carry the soy and heart-disease health claim.

Qualified Health Claims

Where really strong scientific evidence is lacking, the FDA has decided to allow certain "qualified" health claims to be used on the labels of foods and drinks. These are seen as an interim approach that allows producers to inform consumers in a truthful and non-misleading way of the current evidence for products' possible roles in protecting their health.

To be allowed to make such statements, there must be what the FDA considers to be an appropriate level of scientific support. For instance, a qualified claim may state: "Scientific evidence suggests but does not prove . . ." or "Some science shows that a diet high in [this nutrient] may be beneficial, but there is insignificant scientific evidence to prove this effect."

Here are qualified health claims that the FDA has currently confirmed. Many of the products for which approval has been granted are supplements rather than actual foods or drinks.

Qualified Claims about Cancer

— **Selenium:** The FDA acknowledges the possible role that selenium may play in helping reduce the risk of certain human cancers. The organization allows supplements containing this trace mineral to make the following qualified health claims:

- Some scientific evidence suggests that consumption of selenium may reduce the risk of certain forms of cancer. However, [the] FDA has determined that this evidence is limited and not conclusive.

- Some scientific evidence suggests that consumption of selenium may produce anti-carcinogenic effects in the body. However, [the] FDA has determined that this evidence is limited and not conclusive.

The supplement must indicate on its label that there's no benefit in exceeding the tolerable-upper-intake level of 400 mcg per day, and it must contain at least 20 percent or more of the Daily Value (which for selenium is 14 mcg a day).

— **Antioxidant Vitamins:** Dietary supplements containing vitamin E and/or vitamin C may make a qualified claim linking their intake to a reduced risk of cancer:

- Some scientific evidence suggests that consumption of antioxidant vitamins may reduce the risk of certain forms of cancer.

However, [the] FDA has determined that this evidence is limited and not conclusive.

- Some scientific evidence suggests that consumption of antioxidant vitamins may reduce the risk of certain forms of cancer. However, [the] FDA does not endorse this claim because this evidence is limited and not conclusive.

- [The] FDA has determined that although some scientific evidence suggests that consumption of antioxidant vitamins may reduce the risk of certain forms of cancer, this evidence is limited and not conclusive.

The supplement must not recommend or suggest in its labeling (or under ordinary conditions of use) a daily intake exceeding the tolerable upper intake levels established by the Institute of Medicine for vitamin C (2,000 mg per day) or vitamin E (1,000 mg per day), but must supply 20 percent or more of the Daily Value per recommended serving for vitamins C and E (12 mg and 6 IU, respectively).

Qualified Claims about
Cardiovascular Disease

— **Nuts:** There's some evidence suggesting that eating nuts on a regular basis may help lower bad LDL cholesterol and therefore potentially help reduce the risk of heart disease. Therefore, the FDA has allowed some qualified health claims to be made for certain nuts and foods containing them.

This category includes almonds, hazelnuts, peanuts, pecans, some pine nuts, pistachios, and walnuts (see below), none of which contains more than 4 g of saturated fat per 50 g. They may be whole, chopped, blanched, roasted, salted, or lightly coated or flavored. Nut-containing products that have at least 11 g of one or more of these types per serving are also allowed to carry the approved statements.

The claims can read: "Scientific evidence suggests but does not prove that eating 1.5 ounces per day of most nuts, such as [name of specific nut], as part of a diet low in saturated fat and cholesterol may reduce the risk of heart disease."

For whole or chopped nuts (such as a bag of almonds), the claim must be followed by: "(See nutrition information for fat content.)" This is intended to help you realize that nuts are actually a high-fat food, and that eating loads of them will significantly increase your calorie intake. The parenthetical statement doesn't need to be made on nut-containing products, because in order to make any claim, they must have less than 13 g total fat, 4 g saturated fat, 60 mg of cholesterol, and 480 mg of sodium per serving; and they must be a low-saturated-fat and low-cholesterol food. And in addition, they must naturally supply a minimum of 10 percent or more of the Daily Value per serving of vitamin A, vitamin C, iron, calcium, protein, or dietary fiber.

— **Walnuts:** Whole or chopped walnuts have been granted their own special qualified health claim regarding their relationship with heart disease. Packets of these nuts can claim: "Supportive but not conclusive research shows that eating 1.5 ounces per day of walnuts, as part of a low-saturated-fat and low-cholesterol diet and not resulting in increased caloric intake, may reduce the risk of coronary heart disease. See nutrition information for fat [and calorie, optional] content."

It's good that the statement mentions calories, because consuming too many leads to weight gain—which in itself is a risk factor for heart disease!

— **Omega-3 fatty acids:** There's some evidence indicating that the oils in fish such as salmon and sardines and the oil from the liver of whitefish such as cod help keep blood flowing more smoothly, reducing its ability to clot and therefore lowering the risk of heart disease. In acknowledgment of the research available to date, dietary supplements containing the omega-3 long-chain polyunsaturated fatty acids eicosapentaenoic acid (EPA) or docosahexaenoic acid (DHA) have been given permission by the FDA to make this qualified health claim: "Consumption of omega-3 fatty acids may reduce the risk of coronary heart disease. [The] FDA evaluated the data and determined that, although there is scientific evidence supporting the claim, the evidence is not conclusive." The FDA recommends that the products also say that having more than 2 g per day of EPA and DHA isn't recommended.

— **B vitamins:** Some studies indicate that vitamins B_6 and B_{12}, plus the B vitamin folic acid, may help reduce the risk of blood-vessel disease. Given this, the FDA has allowed the following qualified health claim to be made on dietary supplements containing these nutrients: "As part of a well-balanced diet that is low in saturated fat and cholesterol, folic acid, vitamin B_6, and vitamin B_{12} may reduce the risk of vascular disease. [The] FDA evaluated the above claim and found that, while it is known that diets low in saturated fat and cholesterol reduce the risk of heart disease and other vascular diseases, the evidence in support of the above claim is inconclusive."

Any supplements that contain more than 100 percent of the Daily Value of folic acid (400 mcg) must also specify that the safe upper limit for daily intake is 1,000 mcg (1 mg). The type of folic acid used to make the supplement must also meet the United States Pharmacopeia (USP) standards for disintegration and dissolution or be bioavailable within the product.

— Monounsaturated fatty acids from olive oil: Research from around the world reveals that there could be a link between regularly eating these nutrients and a reduced risk of heart disease, which may come from their ability to reduce inflammation on artery walls. The FDA has allowed manufacturers of olive oil to use this qualified health claim: "Limited and not conclusive scientific evidence suggests that eating about 2 tablespoons (23 g) of olive oil daily may reduce the risk of coronary heart disease due to the monounsaturated fat in olive oil. To achieve this possible benefit, olive oil is to replace a similar amount of saturated fat and not increase the total number of calories you eat in a day. One serving of this product contains x grams of olive oil."

Foods that may carry this health claim are:

- All products that are essentially pure olive oil; this includes virgin olive oil and blends of virgin and refined olive oil.

- Salad dressings that contain 6 g or more of olive oil per serving, are low in cholesterol, and don't have more than 4 g of saturated fat per 50 g.

- Vegetable-oil spreads that contain 6 g or more of olive oil per serving, are low in cholesterol, and don't contain more than 4 g of saturated fat per serving.

- Foods containing olive oil (such as sauces or baked goods) that have 6 g or more of olive oil per serving; are low in cholesterol; and contain at least 10% of the Daily Value of either vitamin A, vitamin C, iron, calcium, protein, or dietary fiber. If the serving size is greater than 30 g, then the item can't contain more than 4 g of saturated fat per serving; if it's 30 g or

less, then the food can't contain more than
4 g of saturated fat per 50 g.

- Shortenings with 6 g or more of olive oil per
  serving that are low in cholesterol and don't
  contain more than 4 g of saturated fat.

All isn't lost if a product contains more fat and
saturated fat than these criteria require. If this is the
case, then the package can simply say: "See nutrition information," so you're aware of the actual levels present. Prepared meals and main-dish products,
however, aren't eligible.

Phosphatidylserine and Cognitive Dysfunction . . . and Dementia

Your brain contains large amounts of fatty tissues,
which include substances known as "phospholipids."
These help hold brain cells together and control the
entrance and exit of substances into and out of cells.
One of these, called "phosphatidylserine" (PS), is
especially important in relaying chemical messages
throughout the brain, helping it store and retrieve
information. As humans get older, levels of PS seem

to decline, which may have an impact on the brain's effectiveness.

There's some evidence that taking PS supplements may help restore brainpower. Given this information, the FDA has allowed qualified health claims to be used on food supplements containing PS sourced from soy:

- Consumption of phosphatidylserine may reduce the risk of dementia in the elderly. Very limited and preliminary scientific research suggests that phosphatidylserine may reduce the risk of dementia in the elderly. [The] FDA concludes that there is little scientific evidence supporting this claim.

- Consumption of phosphatidylserine may reduce the risk of cognitive dysfunction in the elderly. Very limited and preliminary scientific research suggests that phosphatidylserine may reduce the risk of cognitive dysfunction in the elderly. [The] FDA concludes that there is little scientific evidence supporting this claim.

Folic Acid and Neural-Tube Birth Defects

As mentioned in the General and Approved Claims section on folate and neural-tube defects, there's evidence that by having sufficient quantities of this B vitamin in their diets, women of childbearing age can reduce the risk of babies being born with defects such as spina bifida.

In addition to the previous statement, the FDA allows a qualified claim on food supplements containing 0.8 mg of folic acid, the synthetic form of folate, which reads: "0.8 mg folic acid in a dietary supplement is more effective in reducing the risk of neural-tube defects than a lower amount in foods in common form. FDA does not endorse this claim. Public-health authorities recommend that women consume 0.4 mg folic acid daily from fortified foods or dietary supplements or both to reduce the risk of neural tube defects."

Keep in Mind . . .

Health claims may seem to be rather vague when they say that a nutrient *may* help prevent this or that disease. This is because while diet plays a role in the development of certain diseases, it often isn't the only cause. So it would be inaccurate to say that by eating a certain food or drink you'll definitely avoid heart disease or develop cancer.

Unlike other countries, the U.S. FDA doesn't allow health claims on foods or drinks that are good in terms of one nutrient (such as fiber), but are also high in fat or salt. The exception to this rule is sugar, for which there are no Daily Values. It's possible for a high-fiber breakfast cereal, for instance, to also be high in sugar, so check the ingredients list. If any type of sugar (including sucrose, glucose, or corn syrup) comes high up in the list, then the product is probably rich in this nutrient, even if it also has a fiber health claim.

Even if you're clear on the hard facts of health claims, words such as *fresh* and *natural* may leave you a little confused. The next chapter will explain exactly what they mean.

* * *

Chapter 5

Fresh, Natural, and Lactose-Free . . . What Do These Terms Mean?

If you've ever looked at a label and seen the words *fresh, natural,* or perhaps *lactose-free* and thought, *Um . . . what exactly does that mean?* then this chapter is for you. You'll find the explanations for some of the most commonly used terms to help you get to the bottom of what they're all about and whether they should influence what you eat and drink.

Fresh

You can be forgiven for thinking that the word *fresh* means just that: a food that's been freshly prepared and is ready for you to sink your teeth into. In fact, this term has been misused in the past, so the FDA has now issued guidelines:

It can be put on the label when it's used to suggest that a food is raw or unprocessed, has never been frozen or heated, and contains no preservatives. Irradiation at low levels, however, is allowed.

While the word by itself may only be used if it accurately describes the product, phrases that incorporate "fresh" and its variations aren't subject to such strict standards.

"Freshly Cooked," "Freshly Prepared," and "Fresh Baked"

These descriptions really do seem to add a dish's "ah" factor. It's hard not to feel warm and happy about such words, and they're very likely to sway your shopping decisions. If it's a toss-up between fresh-baked muffins and some plain old rolls, I know which ones I'd be tempted by!

In reality, although these labels may fire your imagination and get the saliva flowing, they may not mean anything regarding a product's quality. So if you see these expressions, check the period of time and context in which the claim is being used. If, for example, the muffins were baked on the day you're buying them, then that seems fair enough. If they were "freshly baked" yesterday or several days earlier, then these words are a little misleading.

You see, unless bread has genuinely been made from scratch in the store, the use of the description "freshly baked bread" isn't really considered acceptable. Very often these days, bread comes to the store partly baked and is just finished on-site—so loaves prepared in this way shouldn't really be described as "freshly baked," "baked in store," or even "oven fresh."

This may not matter one way or the other to you, as long as what you get is hot and tasty. But if you're a purist, then you may want to ask the manager exactly how the bread is prepared before deciding what to buy.

"Fresh Frozen," "Frozen Fresh," and "Freshly Frozen"

These terms can be used for foods that are quickly frozen while still fresh, such as peas that are harvested and rapidly frozen immediately afterward. It's acceptable for the food to be blanched (scalding it briefly) before freezing to help stop the loss of nutrients like vitamin C.

"Fresh Squeezed" or "Freshly Squeezed"

If a juice has been made from juice concentrates, then the word *fresh* shouldn't be used. If it does qualify for this label, be aware that such drinks usually aren't pasteurized, which is a heating process that takes the liquid to 160° for 15 seconds to help kill any harmful bacteria. Because they haven't undergone this kind of treatment, freshly squeezed unpasteurized juices sold in bottles are generally displayed on ice or in refrigerated cases and must carry a warning on the label saying that the product "may contain harmful bacteria that can cause serious illness in children, the elderly, and persons with weakened immune systems." Untreated, freshly squeezed beverages that are sold by the glass (not in bottles) don't have to carry this warning label.

If a beverage of this type *has* been pasteurized to prolong its shelf life, then the maker should say so on the label by using the words *freshly squeezed pasteurized juice.* It's important, because this kind of heat treatment reduces the amount of vitamin C the juice contains.

"Fresh" Pasta, Soups, and Sauces

You won't find many makers of pasta trying to get away with using the word *fresh* on dried noodles—although you never know! Usually, fresh pasta is the type that needs just a couple of minutes to cook and will only last a few days in the fridge. You'll find it in the refrigerated section of the supermarket.

As for soups and sauces, since there are lots of fresh ones available these days, it's accepted that the word *fresh* can be used to used to describe those that have a relatively short shelf life while refrigerated, compared to more heavily processed versions in cans and bottles.

Natural

This is an interesting claim: Unless it appears on meat or poultry products, there's no standard definition for it. For these exceptions, the word *natural* on the label means that the product doesn't contain any artificial flavorings, colors, chemical preservatives, or artificial or synthetic ingredients. It also guarantees that it's been minimally processed—that is, it hasn't undergone anything that fundamentally altered the raw product.

For all other goods, "natural" is a general claim that implies that the food or its packaging is made from environmentally friendly materials and that nothing artificial or synthetic has been added to the product itself. However, there's currently no standard definition for the term. The best advice is not to be too swayed by this claim, and to study the product closely before assuming that "natural" automatically means "good for you."

Lactose-Free and Reduced Lactose

Lactose is the type of sugar found in milk and to a lesser extent in dairy foods such as yogurt. About 25 percent of the U.S. adult population and 75 percent of adults worldwide are said to digest lactose poorly or have low lactase levels. This means that they don't have sufficient amounts of the enzyme lactase that breaks down lactose, allowing it to be absorbed across the intestinal wall and into the blood.

The result is that the sugar moves undigested into the colon, where it feeds bacteria and leads to the production of potentially painful and embarrassing gas. This condition is common in African Americans, Hispanics, Native Americans, and Asian Americans, who naturally produce little lactase after infancy.

According to the National Diary Council, lactose-reduced milk contains about 70 percent less of this natural sugar than regular milk. Lactose-free milk is 100 percent lactose reduced and is suitable for people with any degree of trouble in this area.

Nondairy

Oddly enough, the term *nondairy* doesn't actually mean that the product is milk-free. In practice, the nondairy creamer that you may use in your coffee can be made from a milk protein called "caseinate." Although this word will appear on the ingredients list, and it will be explained in parentheses that it's a milk derivative, if you're allergic to milk products and rely on the term *nondairy* without checking the ingredients, you could be in trouble. When you see this word on the label, always read the fine print.

Other Terms of Note

While deciphering the meanings of "fresh" and "natural" can be difficult enough, when other seemingly innocuous terms get thrown into the mix, your head can feel like it's spinning. Following are several claims food manufacturers like to make about their products . . . along with the truth behind them.

"Sodium-Free"

Sodium-free is a definition provided by the American Heart Association. Products with fewer than 5 mg of sodium per serving qualify for this label. (See Chapter 6 for more information on the American Heart Association.)

"Gluten-Free"

Gluten is a type of protein found in wheat, oats, and barley that causes the lining of the digestive system to become badly inflamed when eaten by people with celiac disease. This means poor absorption of nutrients and can lead to malnutrition.

It's crucial that people with celiac disease remove all traces of gluten from their diet. There are a growing number of lines of gluten-free foods on the supermarket shelves, including cookies, cakes, breakfast cereals, and crackers made from other grains such as corn and rice so that they can be enjoyed by those on this special diet.

"Free Range"

This is a popular label seen on eggs, chicken, and other meat products. It certainly makes it seem as if the animal has spent a good portion of its life outdoors, grazing, foraging, and running around having a great time.

The reality is rather different. While the USDA has defined "free range" or "free roaming" for poultry that ends up being consumed itself (such as in chicken salad), this isn't the case for hens laying eggs. And even for the birds destined to become turkey burgers, the government only requires that outdoor access be made available for "an undetermined period each day" . . . which means that the coop or stall could be opened for just five minutes each morning! And it gets worse: If the chicken doesn't see the open door or chooses not to dart outside for a quick gulp of fresh air and peck at the ground, it could still qualify as being free range.

"No Hormones Administered"

This broad claim implies that no hormones were used in the production of a food product. The fact is that the USDA prohibits the use of hormones in the raising of hogs and birds within the United States anyway. This means that if pork and poultry products carry this claim, it actually doesn't mean anything, because they shouldn't contain any hormones in the first place.

It's a different story when it comes to cattle, which may be given hormones during their natural life. When beef is labeled "no hormones administered," this is a plus, because the farmer has gone beyond the regulations for conventional meat production.

The label "hormone free," however, is considered to be "unapprovable" on any meat products, and there is currently no standard definition for the term except for "whole meats"—in other words, the claim can be used on a steak, but not on a potpie containing beef. Unless otherwise specified, there's no organization independently certifying this claim. (See Chapter 8 on organic food to find out more about residues in meat.)

May Contain Nut Traces

Approximately four million Americans, including up to 6 percent of all American children, are allergic to one type of food or another. Eight substances are most commonly recognized as being capable of causing reactions:

1.   Peanuts
2.   Milk
3.   Eggs
4.   Fish
5.   Soybeans
6.   Crustaceans
7.   Tree nuts
8.   Wheat

The amount of an allergenic food needed to cause a severe reaction, especially with nuts, can be minimal. For example, consumption of as little as $\frac{1}{5}^{th}$ to $\frac{1}{5,000}^{th}$ of a teaspoon of a trigger can cause death. Thus, what may appear to be an insignificant amount of a food substance to one individual can be potentially lethal for someone else.

Knowing this, it's easy to see just how crucial the labeling of potentially allergenic foods such as nuts really is. Currently, companies are allowed to use the phrase "may contain nuts" on their labels if they can't guarantee that a food they're producing is free of this substance. This is usually because nuts are being used in the same machines for other foods. A company that makes similar foods with and without nuts may have difficulty cleaning the machines in between making the different versions, or packages may run the risk of being mislabeled. This contamination is most likely to occur with cookies, candies, cereals, chocolate, ice cream, dried soups, and nut butters.

Allergen advisories or "May contain" statements have been developed by the food industry and are voluntary. As a result, there's no standardization of messages and no rules for when these warnings can or should appear. Some companies rely on them, others don't; some use them sparingly, others put them on every product. People with allergies to specific foods are urged to seek professional help and to be fully aware of exactly what items are safe for them to consume.

Keep in Mind . . .

As with other claims that you may encounter on food packaging, the issues discussed in this chapter are more helpful if you remember some basic tips:

- If you see descriptions such as "naturally better" or "nature's way," take a step back, because they really don't mean anything.

- Reviewing what the terms *fresh* and *free range* refer to can help you make more informed shopping choices.

- Try not to react emotionally to the words and pictures used on labels—they aren't always what they seem.

- If you need to avoid certain ingredients in products for medical reasons, always err on the side of caution.

Ultimately, if it's quality you're searching for, look beyond all of the descriptions in this chapter and check out the ingredients, where the product comes from, and the proportions of the ingredients used. In the next chapter, you'll get additional tools for making shopping decisions in the form of symbols and logos that can give you more information about a food's nutritional value and origins.

Chapter 6

Symbols and Logos

These days, quite a lot of foods and beverages carry small symbols, logos, and endorsements. You may have seen a red heart with a white check mark through it (the "heart check" of the American Heart Association) on breakfast cereal or margarine, or the fair-trade logo on coffee or tea.

What do these logos actually mean? Well, this depends on whose image it is. There's no such thing as an FDA-approved logo, so it's a bit of a free-for-all. Most symbols fall into two broad categories: those regarding health and those related to ecological and humanitarian concerns. What they signify depends on the morals and ethics of the organization to which they belong.

This chapter looks at some of the ones you're most likely to come across, with explanations of the criteria foods and drinks need to meet to display them. Once you're in the know, you can decide if these marks should be influencing your shopping list.

Logos of Well-Known Health Organizations

The first set of images we'll look at were created and are issued by nationally respected groups concerned with promoting better health for all Americans.

American Heart Association

The American Heart Association is a national voluntary health agency whose mission is to reduce disability and death from cardiovascular diseases and stroke. It was started in 1924 by six American cardiologists in New York City and is now based in Dallas.

The organization carries out a wide range of work that helps spread information about preventing and treating heart disease. One of the most effective ways they do this is through the use of their "heart check."

If a label carries this mark, it means that it's met the American Heart Association's Food Certification

Program's core values, which were established in 1995 to provide you with an easy and reliable way to spot products that are healthy for your heart. This means that any product bearing the "heart check" mark has been thoroughly evaluated and deemed to meet these strict standards of healthiness (per serving):

- Low fat: 3 g or less of fat

- Low saturated fat: 1 g or less of saturated fat

- Low cholesterol: 20 mg or less of cholesterol

- 480 mg or less of sodium (for individual foods)

- At least 10 percent of the Daily Value of one or more of these nutrients in a naturally occurring form: protein, vitamin A, vitamin C, calcium, iron, or dietary fiber

When it comes to seafood, meat, and poultry products, the nutritional standards are slightly different. To get the American Heart Association seal of approval, they must meet the following nutritional requirements per standard serving and per 100 g:

- Less than 5 g of total fat

- Less than 2 g of saturated fat

- Less than 95 mg of cholesterol

- At least 10 percent of the Daily Value of one or more of these nutrients in a naturally occurring form: protein, vitamin A, vitamin C, calcium, iron, or dietary fiber

You can check out which products carry this logo by going to **www.amhrt.org** and clicking on the "Heart-Healthy Grocery Shopping Made Easy" link, where you'll be guided to a personal shopping list of logo-bearing foods.

It's important to bear in mind that the Food Certification Program of the American Heart Association is designed for healthy people over the age of two. Anyone with a medical condition is advised to contact their physician or registered dietitian before making dietary changes.

American Diabetes Association

Founded in 1940, the American Diabetes Association is the nation's leading nonprofit health organization providing diabetes research, information, and advocacy. It has numerous programs running in all 50 states and the District of Columbia.

Its mission is simple: to prevent and cure diabetes, and to improve the lives of all people affected by the disease. The group helps support the more than 18 million people across America who are currently living with diabetes in many ways. One of the most effective is through the use of its logo on products that meet their criteria as being healthy and suitable for people with this condition.

The standards are based on foods eaten in reasonable amounts as either a main dish or an individual serving. Products that are given the okay should meet the FDA's criteria for being low in saturated fat. Typical servings should be modest in both calories and fat and have 1 g or less of saturated fat per serving (or 1 g or less per 100 g if it's a main dish or meal). Because of the wide variety of foods that are commercially available, the group uses the FDA criteria as guidelines rather than rigid standards.

The bottom line is that if a product bears the American Diabetes Association logo, it will be basically healthy, and you won't go wrong in choosing it.

American Dental Association (ADA)

The American Dental Association is a professional society, and about 70 percent of all dentists in America are members. Since 1931, the association has had a Seal of Acceptance, which they permit on products that are considered to be safe and effective. Although 60 percent of these items are for professionals only, such as antibiotics or restorative materials used in a dentist's day-to-day work, the remaining 40 percent are on sale to the general public.

You're probably familiar with the "ADA Accepted" box, having spotted it on things such as toothpaste, dental floss, mouthwash, and toothbrushes. Obviously, none of these are actually foods or drinks, but since you can purchase them at the grocery store, it's worth knowing what this endorsement means.

It's an entirely voluntary program, but more than 300 companies have signed on to it, and the presence of this symbol means that you can rest assured that the product won't be damaging to your teeth or gums.

Ecological and Humanitarian Logos

Most symbols not sponsored by major health organizations have something to do with how or where a product was manufactured.

"Fair Trade"

If you see the fair-trade logo on a label, then you know that the farmers who produced the food or drink were paid a fair price for their efforts. This is a label indicating social responsibility and doesn't claim in any way to be an indication of nutritional content or have any bearing on health.

At the moment, TransFair USA certifies fair-trade coffee and tea. To gain the logo, goods must have been grown by small farmers who belong to cooperatives. A minimum fair price is set for their beans and tea, 60 percent of which is paid in advance of purchase to help reduce the farmers' exposure to the volatile nature of these markets.

By choosing products with the fair-trade logo, you know that you're helping TransFair continue their efforts in creating an alternative economic model, which is attempting to protect the market and improve and encourage the long-term self-reliance of small-scale farmers. You're doing your part to protect vital ecosystems throughout the developing world and strengthen rural communities.

Keep in mind, however, that while a logo such as the "heart mark" gives an indication of a food's healthfulness, the fair-trade logo only refers to the item's production heritage. It doesn't necessarily equal "good for you." Fair-trade chocolate is still a high-fat, high-sugar, high-calorie food.

"Certified Humane Raised and Handled"

If you care about the way animals are treated, then look for the "Certified humane raised and handled" logo. It's designed to guarantee that animals raised for dairy, lamb, poultry, and beef products are treated in a humane manner. This means access to clean and sufficient food and water and a safe and healthful environment from the time animals are born until they're slaughtered. Growth hormones are prohibited under this program, and the diet is free of antibiotics (although such drugs are allowed if the animal is actually sick).

The certification program was developed by a

team of animal scientists and veterinarians that make up the group's scientific committee, and were based in part on the Royal Society for the Prevention of Cruelty to Animals standards developed in the United Kingdom.

You can also be sure that producers who sign up for this endorsement have complied with certain environmental guidelines, such as the American Meat Institute Standards, which has higher criteria than the Federal Humane Slaughter Act. All farms wishing to be certified must pass an inspection. Examiners have training and education in animal science, veterinary medicine, or other relevant backgrounds, and several are also members of the scientific committee. In addition, the USDA's Agricultural Marketing Service (AMS) Livestock and Seed Program verifies the inspection process.

"Dolphin Safe"

No one yet understands quite why, but schools of yellowfin tuna that swim in the eastern tropical Pacific Ocean often choose to do so underneath large groups of dolphins. This is a problem for the dolphins, because when fishermen want to catch the tuna, one of the easiest ways for them to locate a school is to simply check out where the dolphins are. Once they've located the target, they then lower small speedboats into the water from their huge trawlers and chase the dolphins (with the tuna still swimming underneath) until they get tired and stressed.

Next, they drop purse-seine nets into the water, which encircle both groups. While this is an effective way of catching the tuna, the dolphins are traumatized by the chase, the engines, the shouting of the fishermen, and the general mayhem going on around them—and they're often unable to muster the energy to escape. They get hauled aboard the trawlers and are frequently left to die or hurled back into the ocean as good as dead. Up until 1972, as many as half a million dolphins were dying every year as a result of this kind of tuna fishing.

By the late 1980s, a consumer-pressure group led to the development of the "Dolphin safe" label, which has been adopted by major tuna-producing companies in the U.S. To qualify for this logo in the '80s, fishermen had to be able to prove that they caught their tuna without the deliberate setting of nets on dolphins. By 1994, the entire American tuna fleet was deemed to be catching tuna in a dolphin-safe manner, and the U.S. Marine Mammal Protection

Act banned the importation of tuna caught by countries that didn't adhere to these practices.

Tragically, nations such as Mexico, Venezuela, and Colombia continued to fish using the old methods, and they complained that the new laws violated free-trade requirements. The U.S. government responded, and under the ill-named International Dolphin Conservation Act of 1997, the legislation was watered down so that tuna could carry the symbol even if the same old methods were used, as long as dolphins didn't actually die in the process. At best, this meant that the creatures could still be traumatized, shocked, and suffer terrible injuries. They just didn't end up dying in the process. And it could be said that if the onboard observer turned a blind eye—who knows? Maybe many still died.

Since 1997, there's been a running battle between conservation groups and the government to ensure that the strictest and highest standards be reinstated to protect dolphins against tuna-fishing practices that so barbarically affect them. If you want to find out more about the current state of affairs, log on to the Humane Society of the United States at **www.hsus.org** and only buy tuna caught by U.S companies.

"Protected Harvest"

If you're concerned about the level and variety of pesticides used during the growth of crops, then keep an eye out for the "Protected Harvest" certification program logo. (Currently, it only appears on potatoes.) This endeavor aims to reduce the use of pesticides through the use of processes such as weed and insect management; control of insects and disease; and ensuring good soil, water, and harvest management.

Potato growers must be able to prove that their farming methods meet the required standards in these and other areas of production and apply to the organization's certifying body in order to be able to use the logo on their potatoes. Pesticide toxicity is also assessed and certain chemicals are explicitly prohibited. Protected Harvest also has an explicit policy banning the use of genetic engineering.

The standards in place were set through the collaboration of the World Wildlife Fund, the Wisconsin Potato and Vegetable Growers Association, and the University of Wisconsin; and verified by the Great Lakes Agricultural Research Services. At the moment only the "Healthy Grown" brand of potatoes is certified by Protected Harvest, but it's hoped that more producers will join.

"Rainforest Alliance"

The Rainforest Alliance is a nonprofit organization based in New York City with offices throughout the U.S. and worldwide. It aims to promote a sustainable and eco-friendly approach to everything from farming to tourism and forestry in rain-forest areas.

If a food or drink label tells you that it's been grown by a farmer who's certified by the Rainforest Alliance, then there are certain criteria that will have been met during its production that benefit both the farmers and the environment. The organization ensures that certified farmers grow their crops using environmentally responsible management practices, which involve integrated pest- and disease-management practices, the banning of certain pesticides, soil and water conservation, fair labor and minimum-pay practices, and good community relations, all of which have been specifically tailored to crops in specific regions.

Presently, the Rainforest Alliance certifies coffee, banana, cocoa, and orange production. Some 474 farms and cooperatives and 65,009 hectares in Brazil, Costa Rica, Colombia, Ecuador, Guatemala, Honduras, Nicaragua, Panama, the Philippines, Hawaii, Mexico, and El Salvador are part of the program.

More than 50,000 farming families benefit from the practices it promotes.

Fair trade, mentioned earlier in this chapter, is an alternative marketing system designed to give disadvantaged farmers a guaranteed price for their products; it focuses on the ways in which small farmers are organized and on how agricultural products are *traded.* Rainforest Alliance standards, on the other hand, promote sustainable farm *management.* This group works with all farms, from small cooperatives and family spreads to plantations owned by multinational companies, with the aim to promote change at many levels, ensuring benefits for all agricultural workers.

Wildlife conservation is an integral part of this sustainable farm-management system. Guidelines help protect wildlife, forests, and other valuable habitats in and around agricultural areas. Certified coffee and cocoa farms in natural-forest zones, for example, must have diverse shade cover from native trees, which provide a habitat for everything from birds to monkeys. This means that certified farms can quite literally be a haven for wildlife.

The certification process assists farmers by increasing efficiency, reducing costly inputs, and improving management. Workers benefit from a cleaner, safer, and more dignified workplace where their rights are respected. Certified farmers have better access to specialty buyers, contract stability, favorable credit options, publicity, technical assistance, and premium markets. Most are able to utilize their certification to receive a price premium.

With more and more shoppers looking for ecologically sensitive labels and demanding groceries from responsibly managed farms, the Rainforest Alliance label will no doubt play a more and more important role in future shopping decisions.

Keep in Mind . . .

If you understand exactly what various symbols and logos mean, they can be useful. As with most food labeling, knowledge gives you the power to make informed choices and minimizes your chances of being misled. And don't worry: You don't usually pay more for foods that carry symbols and logos—manufacturers should absorb the cost of acquiring them. A category that can get expensive quickly, however, is the subject of the next chapter: children's food.

* * *

Chapter 7

Children's Food

The whole issue of children's food is a fascinating and timely one. Parents are, quite appropriately, getting more and more worried about the types and quantities of foods and drinks that are being marketed directly to their families.

I'm sure you're familiar with the ones I'm thinking of: They include everything from chicken nuggets and burgers to products specially designed for lunch boxes, to items such as sugar-packed yogurt that's plastered with cartoon characters. Such foods are so much a part of our lives these days that it took a chef friend of mine to give the subject a sense of perspective by making the simple comment that "children's food" is a relatively new invention—the younger set used to eat the same food as adults. Now it's not unusual to see a mom making one meal for the kids and another for the grown-ups. In fact, the kitchen has become like a mini restaurant in many homes, with parents having somehow gotten themselves into the position of having to cook special dishes for different people according to their daily whims.

Today, food geared to children is big business, and with this growth has come lots of potential problems for the younger generation's health, in both the short and the long term. In this chapter, I hope you'll be able to step back and understand why this is the case. You'll see how paying close attention to labels can help you choose things that will be good for your children, without ruining all the fun they associate with the brightly packaged products designed to tempt them.

Let's start at the beginning—with babies.

Infant Formula

The FDA has set very specific methods of manufacturing that makers of infant formula have to stick to. This ensures both the safety and nutritional quality. If you look carefully on every container of formula milk for infants, you'll find a code. Extremely detailed records of production and analysis are made with each batch so that every single container can be traced by this code if necessary.

It's required by law that every formula sold in the United States provide minimum levels of 29 essential nutrients, and there are maximum levels set for 9 of them. These can only change if the FDA decides that doing so is necessary and beneficial for babies in the light of new research. The nutrients that must be included are protein, fat, and essential fatty acids, plus a range of vitamins and minerals. All of these are listed on the label. Infant formulas are prohibited from containing additives and colorings.

Baby Food

Once a child begins to eat solid foods, the laws that protect infant formulas and specific weaning foods (such as some baby cereals) just vanish into thin air. When a child can eat, the fact is that they can have anything as far as the law is concerned. This would be fine if everyone still ate the basic food that their parents and grandparents knew: straight-forward meat, vegetables, fruit, grilled or baked fish, and homemade desserts.

Not many people eat like that anymore. Instead, they often rely on processed foods; and these can contain additives, colorings, and unlimited salt just like adult options, but which are forbidden in formula. The only difference between these baby foods and adult fare is that the labels vary slightly.

To begin with, the labels of foods intended for children younger than four years of age have to list specific details for every ingredient. For instance, it's not good enough for manufacturers to simply put "spices" they way they can on adult foods and drinks; instead, they must say precisely which spice is used. Similar guidelines apply to oil: The package can't just declare "vegetable oil"; it must tell exactly which one is being used, such as "sunflower oil." The nutrition-facts format is also different from the adult version, and there are specific guidelines for two age groups: "under two" and "under four."

Under Two Years Old

— **Serving size:** Thank goodness that the serving sizes found in the nutrition-facts box are based on the average amount for a child under the age of two to consume at one sitting, rather than being based on an adult serving size. For example, it could be one-quarter cup of oatmeal, compared to an adult serving of one-half cup of oatmeal, which would be appropriate for a grown-up.

— **Total fat:** This is given per serving, but unlike on the adult label, the calories aren't provided. This is so that parents aren't put off by foods that appear to be relatively fatty, because small children shouldn't have their fat intakes strictly limited before they're two years old. Adequate fat is needed for optimal growth and development.

— **Saturated fat, cholesterol, polyunsaturated fat, and monounsaturated fat:** No information is allowed for any of these fats on foods for children younger than two.

— **Sodium, potassium, total carbohydrates, fiber, sugars, and protein:** Amounts are given for these nutrients.

— **% Daily Values:** These are only listed for protein, vitamins, and minerals. They aren't provided for other nutrients because the dietary guidelines for Americans don't apply to children this young.

Under Four Years Old

— **Total fat:** The nutrition facts can provide information on both the total fat and the percent of calories from fat in the product.

— **Saturated fat and cholesterol:** Levels for both of these can be given on foods for this age group.

— **Sodium, potassium, total carbohydrates, fiber, sugars, and protein:** Amounts for these nutrients are provided.

— **% Daily Values:** With the exception of protein, vitamins, and minerals, these percentages don't appear on items intended for children younger than four, because no Daily Values for nutrients such as sodium exist for this age group.

Making Sense of the Label

One of the main problems with the labeling of foods and drinks for children younger than age four (and age two) is that parents can't easily see whether something is high, medium, or low in terms of the amount of sodium and sugar it supplies.

Sodium

Too much sodium is a particular problem for small children whose kidneys, which excrete excess amounts of sodium from the body, aren't properly formed. While infant formula and baby foods intended for children younger than one year have strict limitations on sodium levels, as soon as a child passes his or her first birthday, sodium intake can soar—and unfortunately, it often does.

To help you interpret the levels of this mineral in children's foods, it's well worth looking at the levels recommended by the National Academy of Sciences. They've set a limit of 325 to 975 mg of sodium a day as being adequate and safe for children from one to three years old.

If you take a look at some products marketed specifically to this age group, you'll be alarmed to discover that many have 500 to 700 mg of sodium per serving. This means that in just one helping, a child can be getting close to the upper limit for the whole day. The FDA and USDA, who specifically regulate the content of toddler products containing meat, are working with manufacturers to sort out this problem. Let's hope they make some serious headway—and soon.

For your reference, here are the sodium-consumption levels recommended for children from ages 1 to 13-plus, as suggested by the National Academy of Sciences.

Daily Values				
Age of child	**1–3**	**4–8**	**9–13**	**Older than 13**
Sodium per day	1.5 g 1,500 mg	1.9 g 1,900 mg	2.2 g 2,200 mg	2.3 g 2,300 mg

The Center for Science in the Public Interest is a nonprofit organization based in Washington, D.C., that works to improve the public's health through its work on nutrition, food safety, and alcohol. It's issued some guidelines to encourage responsible marketing of food designed specifically for children:

- No more than 150 mg of sodium per serving of chips, cereal, crackers, cheese, baked goods, French fries, and other snack items

- No more than 480 mg of sodium for soups, pastas, meats, and main dishes

- No more than 600 mg of sodium for entire meals

Sugar

There isn't a Daily Value for sugar for adults in the U.S., let alone for children. This means that unless you can interpret what the grams mean in the context of a daily diet, the figure in the nutrition-facts section of the label will probably mean very little to you.

The Center for Science in the Public Interest is calling for manufacturers of children's foods and drinks to have less than 25 percent of calories come from added sugars. By this they mean sucrose (table sugar), maple syrup, glucose, and the like; natural sugars from any fruit or dairy in the product don't count toward this percentage. To put this into context, if a cup of yogurt provides 150 calories, it should have no more than 9 g of added sugars, but many contain double this amount.

It's important to keep in mind that the general advice on healthy eating still holds true: Sugars don't add any nutrients to a child's diet and are a source of empty calories. It's best to limit their intake.

For more, highly detailed information, visit **www. cfsan.fda.gov/~dms/flg-5-2.html.**

Given the limits of these labels, you can see why it's even more important that you become a real label detective when you're shopping for children. The reason that the levels of salt and additives are restricted in foods intended for infants is because their liver and kidneys, which have to deal with detoxifying these substances, are immature and simply can't cope. It seems a little strange that, having reached the age of one, these organs are immediately supposed to be able to manage much higher levels—or that from this point on in life, little children are fair game to be exposed to products rich in sugar and fat. (See sample Nutrition-Facts labels on page 168.)

Marketing and Promotion

The only way to ensure that children are eating healthful and nutritious food appropriate for their age is to go back to basics as much as possible and cut down on processed foods. This can be very difficult when junk food is peddled to them from the moment they wake until they crash into bed at night. After all, it's human nature to be drawn to brightly colored foods and packaging.

Fruits and vegetables brilliantly fulfill the role of brightening up mealtimes. Wander through the produce section of any supermarket and you'll see them naturally packaged in every color under the sun: red strawberries and tomatoes, indigo eggplants and berries, yellow bananas and corn, orange carrots and tangerines, and green apples and spinach . . . the possibilities go on and on. Having plenty of these items on the table has brought vibrancy to meals over the centuries, but these days, it isn't just nature's bounty adding new hues to our daily diet.

Colors are used to great effect, not just in foods to make them look appetizing, but also on packaging and labels to stimulate and attract attention. Products aimed at children make full use of color on their packages and labels to make sure they trigger the "I want" button, getting children to nag, cajole, bargain, whine, throw tantrums, and bully their parents into putting these things into the shopping cart.

But it isn't just the colors that inspire such behavior. Lots of other packaging tactics are employed with great success to get you to load your cupboards with food just for kids, and once again in the label game, knowledge is power. Food and drink manufacturers don't leave things to chance. Many employ child psychologists to find out exactly how to turn kids on, and they organize focus groups, in which they test their ideas on real children and get their opinions on what would and wouldn't make them want to eat or drink certain products.

Here are a couple of the most blatant ways that products are marketed to children through their packaging:

- Advertising the presence of a free gift inside with big letters across the label. This is common on breakfast cereals.

- Featuring pictures of celebrities such as athletes and movie stars, along with favorite cartoon characters, to capture little fans' attention. These may appear on cans of cola, bags of chips, and (again) breakfast cereals.

Away from the actual products, manufacturers use other tactics that dovetail with what's in the store:

- Advertising on television and through new media like the Internet, text messaging, and e-mail newsletters in order to sow the seed and then remind children that they want the food or drink.

- Also using celebrities and cartoon characters on advertising and promotional material to create the "I want" feeling in children's minds.

- Tying special promotions to schools, such as collecting a certain number of wrappers so that the school can trade them in for sports equipment, books, or computers. Chip and candy manufacturers are big fans of these schemes.

The Impact on Children

Many of us are aware that over the last few years, children have been getting fatter and fatter. In fact, there's now twice the number of obese children—and three times the number of obese teens—as existed just 20 years ago. Even considering those who do manage to stay at a normal body weight, only 2 percent actually eat nutritious meals.

In most cases, children's diets are too high in calories, saturated and trans fats, refined sugars, and salt; and too low in fruits, vegetables, whole grains, and calcium. The problem is that these trends increase the risk of heart disease, cancer, diabetes, and osteoporosis. This is serious stuff.

As a direct result of the lousy things they're consuming, 25 percent of children between five and ten years old have high blood pressure and cholesterol that's above safe levels. Many are now also developing type 2 diabetes, which used to be a disease that mostly affected overweight adults in later life.

Marketing Guidelines

The Center for Science in the Public Interest has issued some guidelines to encourage responsible marketing of food to children. They hope that everyone—food manufacturers, restaurants, supermarkets, television and radio stations, movie studios, magazines, public-relations and advertising agencies, schools, toy and video-game manufacturers, and organizers of sporting events—will use these standards to rethink their promotions for children.

— **Beverages:** Low-nutrition drinks shouldn't be marketed to children, period. These include sugar-laden soft drinks, sports drinks, punch, iced tea, and any others with less than 50 percent real juice. (In my opinion, there's no reason that children shouldn't just drink water and low-fat milk along with 100 percent fruit juice, although the latter two should be had in moderation.)

— **Foods:** Low-nutrition foods shouldn't be marketed to children either. The usual culprits are most fast foods, chips, sweets, and the like.

— **Reformulation:** The Center wants products aimed at children to be reformulated to have more fruits, vegetables, and whole grains in them, while reducing the portion sizes, calories, sodium, refined sugars, and saturated and trans fats in those items already out there.

— **Television advertising:** Nutritionally poor choices shouldn't be advertised during television shows for which more than a quarter of the viewers are children.

— **Movies and other media:** Low-nutrition products also shouldn't be promoted during movies or video games; or in Websites, books, and textbooks.

We can only hope that manufacturers make the decision to follow these guidelines. It's odd to think that in a society where there are very specific laws to protect other aspects of children's health—such as those governing car seats and cigarettes—it's considered okay to market junk food to them day and night, even though it can set them up for many health problems.

Guiding Young Lives

While there are myriad methods used to tempt children to buy or badger their parents to get such low-nutrition foods and drinks, it's the label itself that often begins the process of seduction. Manufacturers need to take a long, hard look at what they're putting in their products for children. Improvement in content could then be proudly brought to our attention through one of the most powerful marketing tools of all, the food label. Until then, responsible adults need to be on guard.

You are what you eat, and this is especially true for children, who are growing and developing so rapidly. Food contains nutrients that build bones and keep the heart pumping and the brain developing to its maximum capacity.

Since this is the case, do you really want your child's body to be an internal mishmash of additives, fat, and sugar? Should they be developing weak bones and teeth, maintaining hyper energy levels, and getting excess fat deposited on their tummies, bottoms, arms, and legs? Poor nutrition even increases the chances of them dying before you do because their arteries have been clogged with saturated and trans fats. The heart can be put under just so much strain through excess weight that it gives up; and the pancreas packs it in when it's unable to cope with the sugar burden, leading to diabetes, kidney disease, and blindness.

If this horrifies you, then you really do need to be prescriptive. You need to conquer "pester power" and buy the foods that you know to be good for them. Forget people telling you that there's no such things as a bad food—there is. The poor choices are packed with additives, fat, and sugar and are devoid of nutrients. Although a small quantity every once in a while won't do any harm, the point is that kids don't eat small quantities anymore. Bad foods have become daily features in the diets of many children, and as such, are doing them harm in both the short and the long term.

But while it's a good idea to get children back to eating real food, it's also important not to turn them into total health freaks. Children younger than two, for example, should be given whole milk. Two percent is fine from ages two to five, but parents shouldn't go overboard with low-fat foods that are full of fiber. Getting back to basics with simple meals and having snacks of fruit and yogurt will help keep the balance.

This page of the American Dietetic Association's Website contains detailed and technical dietary guidance for healthy children aged 2 to 11 years: **www. eatright.org/Public/Other/index_adap0199.cfm.** When in doubt, however, check with your doctor for information about your child's needs.

Frequently Asked Questions (FAQs)

Q. If drinks marketed to children are full of sugar, then aren't they just liquid candy?

A. In a nutshell, yes. A typical 12-ounce bottle of orange drink that has the nerve to boast on its label that it's "rich in vitamin C," contains a shocking 70 g of sugar. To give this some perspective, that's 14 teaspoons, equivalent to the sugar found in seven lollipops—more than a child's recommended maximum-sugar intake for a whole day. Do your kids a favor: Wean them off these things and get them drinking water instead.

Q. Should the advertising of junk food to children be banned?

A. There's no doubt that advertising and marketing high-sugar and high-fat sweets and snacks to children has an impact. Here are the most effective strategies—although they aren't always the easiest!

- Minimize television-viewing time in order to reduce exposure to commercials.

- Leave children at home when grocery shopping so that they aren't in the direct fire of clever marketing on products in the store.

- If it's available in your area, try shopping online and having the groceries delivered.

Combine this with healthy eating practices at home and leading by example, and you have a good chance of minimizing the potential damage caused by the marketing of low-nutrition products to children and teens.

Q. Is it true that fast-food chains add things to their French fries to make them tastier—and therefore more appealing to children?

A. It's true that some chains add dextrose (a form of sugar) to their fries, ostensibly to make them yellow. Then salt is often sprinkled on before serving, which encourages you to buy more beverage.

It's also good to be aware that fast-food chains have been known to specifically design their offerings so that they hardly need any chewing, which makes them very quick to eat. The faster something can be gobbled, the less likely children are to feel satisfied by it, and the more likely they are to want more. It's clever marketing.

My advice is to absolutely minimize trips to burger joints; if you do go, take advantage of the healthier offerings now available, such as chicken-pita wraps. Making healthy versions at home, such as extra-lean burgers with lots of tomatoes, lettuce, and vegetable toppings, is another option.

Keep in Mind . . .

- Always look at the list of ingredients. (Review Chapter 2 for explanations of how to read and make sense of this part of the label.)

- Infant formulas must stick to strict nutritional and compositional guidelines regarding additives.

- Food aimed at children over age one is unregulated when it comes to nutritional content and the use of additives. Many products are high in fat, sugar, salt, and calories.

- Check the nutrition information, and remember that children don't need adult servings. If foods look high in troublesome nutrients, it's probably better that children eat them infrequently.

- It's crucial for parents and caretakers to take control of children's diets and help kids establish healthy-eating habits for life. Eating well yourself is the one surefire way you have of teaching good habits by example.

Many of us take our concern about food quality—for ourselves and our families—to the next level, which is the subject of Chapter 8: organic food.

* * *

Example of Label for a Fruit Dessert for Children Younger Than Two:

Example of a Label for a Fruit Dessert for Children Ages Two to Four:

Organic Food

Sales of organic food have rocketed over the last decade, and this trend looks set to continue. Whether you want to buy it for moral, environmental, or health reasons, you need to know how to tell if something actually is organic! And this, of course, means that you have to rely on labeling.

The aim of organic farmers is to produce food while maximizing the health of the environment and the animals on the farms. In doing so, they reduce pollution and soil erosion, increase biodiversity and sustainability, use less energy, and work with animals that are as stress free as possible.

Pesticides and artificial fertilizers are kept to an absolute minimum, and permitted fertilizers are made without synthetic ingredients, sewage sludge, bioengineering, or ionizing radiation. Veterinary products used in animal husbandry are also minimal, which means that organic meat, eggs, and dairy products come from animals that aren't routinely given antibiotics and growth hormones. As far as the consumer is concerned, the end products contain negligible residues of pesticides and herbicides.

Let's begin by taking a look at the regulations for this part of the food industry.

Standards and Certification

Unlike almost all other foods, which are regulated by the Food and Drug Administration, organic products are under the jurisdiction of the United States Department of Agriculture—specifically the Organic Foods Production Act and the National Organic Program. These laws are intended to assure customers that the foods labeled as "organic" have been produced, processed, and certified to consistent national standards.

This fixed set of rules was issued in December 2002. It took ten years to develop them, and they must be met by anyone using the organic label in the United States. Certifying organizations may not alter them in any way, and any conflicts of interest must be disclosed.

Certifying Organizations

The USDA regulations require that everyone who produces and handles foods and products that carry an organic claim must be certified by one of their accredited certification agencies. The only exceptions to this rule are for small farms or handlers who sell less than $5,000 in gross-organic sales, handlers that buy and sell without repackaging or changing the product's form, and retailers that don't process food.

There are many certifying organizations that have accreditation from the USDA. Seals or symbols from any of these groups signal to consumers that the farmers and producers have met all the rigorous standards set by the USDA National Organic Program (USDA NOP):

- **American Food Safety Institute** (since 2003)
- **Global Organic Alliance (GOA)** (since 1997)
- **Natural Food Certifiers** (since 2002)

If you see another organic certification on a package, check to make sure that they're following the USDA NOP standards.

Imported Goods

In order to market agricultural products as organic in the United States, imported foods and drinks carrying that label must have been produced and handled in accordance with the Organic Foods Production Act and the National Organic Program.

The USDA is presently working with many governments overseas to ensure that their individual organic-certifying agencies meet domestic standards. Countries that already conform include Canada, Denmark, Israel, New Zealand, Spain, and the United Kingdom. Evaluations are currently taking place to determine whether the programs of India, Japan, Australia, and the European Union are equivalent to American standards.

Labeling Terms

Manufacturers can make a variety of claims using the word *organic*, and there are different guidelines for each approved uses of this desirable term. In every case, the name and address of the final product's organic-certifying agent must be printed on the information panel so that consumers have the ability to contact them.

"Organic"

In order to qualify for this label, the item must consist of at least 95 percent organically produced ingredients, although salt and water are excluded from this requirement. Any remaining nonorganic components must be nonagricultural substances that are on the USDA's approved national list or be nonorganic agricultural products that simply don't have a commercially available organic form.

Products bearing this designation must state their credentials on the principal display panel and must not have been created using excluded methods of production, sewage sludge, or ionizing radiation.

"100 Percent Organic"

To be able to claim that it's 100 percent organic, an item must quite simply be made entirely from organically produced ingredients, although water and salt are again excluded from this requirement.

Just as with organic goods, products bearing this designation must state their credentials on the principal display panel and must not have been created using excluded methods of production, sewage sludge, or ionizing radiation.

"Made with Organic Ingredients"

If a product such as a loaf of bread contains some organic ingredients, it can state that it's "made with organic ingredients," as long as at least 70 percent of the total components meet organically produced standards. To use this expression, the food or drink must then list up to three of the organic ingredients or food groups on the principal display panel. For example, soup made with at least 70 percent organic ingredients and only organic vegetables may be labeled either "soup made with organic peas, potatoes, and carrots," or "soup made with organic vegetables."

Products containing less than 70 percent organic material can't use the term *organic* anywhere on the principal display panel, but they may identify the specific items that are organically produced in the ingredients list on the information panel.

Organic Animals

Organically raised livestock (such as cattle, pigs, and hens) may not be given hormones to promote growth, or receive antibiotics for any reason if they're healthy. However, if they become ill, they must be given medicine, since this is only fair and humane. But if they're treated with a drug prohibited by the USDA NOP, then food made from these animals can't go on to be sold as organic. They may be given vitamin and mineral supplements and approved vaccinations, but as you can imagine, there are strict guidelines regarding the administration of both.

A positive part of animal welfare in organic farming is that creatures must have access to the outdoors, including access to pastures for cattle. The only times during which animals may be temporarily confined is if they're ill, for their own safety, when reproducing, and to protect the soil or the quality of their water supply. Otherwise, unlike much livestock farmed in commercial systems, organic animals live relatively normal lives as nature intended.

Animals bred for slaughter (such as sheep and cattle) must be raised under "organic management," which means that all of these rules apply to them from the last third of their gestation period. For poultry, the appropriate conditions can begin no later than the second day of life.

All must be given agricultural food products that are 100 percent organic. Producers may convert an entire, distinct dairy herd to organic production by providing 80 percent organically produced feed for nine months, followed by three months of 100 percent organically produced feed.

Nutrition Claims for Organic Foods

Since they're grown without many chemicals, do organic fruits and vegetables contain more nutrients than nonorganic versions? This is a tricky issue. While large studies are now under way, there's already some research that suggests that the nutritional value of organic foods may be greater than nonorganic equivalents. Some studies do show that levels of vitamin C and the antioxidant beta-carotene can be higher in organic potatoes and carrots.

Others show that minerals such as calcium and magnesium are better in organic apples, and there's good scientific work revealing that the levels of essential omega-3 fatty acids (a nutrient that helps keep blood thin and reduces inflammation) in organic whole milk are higher than standard milk because the cows have grazed on real grass, which naturally contains omega-3s. Organic milk could therefore be a useful addition to your diet, returning a natural source of this nutrient, which has declined over the last 100 years.

More work needs to be done in this area, and there are studies under way. In some aspects, I feel that it doesn't particularly matter if an organic potato has a few more milligrams of vitamin C. The other issues, such as pesticide residues, environmental issues, and a person's moral views about whether or not to go organic, are probably much more important in the decision-making process.

Additives in Organic Foods

As you'd expect, there are some strict guidelines regarding which additives can be used in organically certified foods and drinks. The entire list is published in a document called "The Organic Foods Production Act's National List of Allowed and Prohibited Substances." Even if you don't feel like cracking that tome, you'll get a good feel for just how strict the guidelines are if you read these points outlining the conditions where synthetic additives can be used:

- Equivalents genuinely can't be produced from a natural source, and there are absolutely no organic substitutes.

- The manufacture, use, and disposal of the synthetic additive doesn't have an adverse effect on the environment and is done in a manner compatible with organic handling.

- The nutritional quality of the food is maintained, and the synthetic additive or any of its breakdown products don't have adverse health effects.

- The primary use isn't as a preservative; and it isn't being added to re-create or improve flavors, colors, textures, or nutritive value lost during processing, except where the replacement of nutrients is required by law (such as folic acid in flour used for making bread).

- It's "Generally Recognized As Safe" (GRAS) by the FDA and is only used in a way that meets the FDA's "Good Manufacturing Practices."

- It contains no residues of heavy metals or other contaminants in excess of tolerances set by the FDA.

- It's essential for the handling of organically produced agricultural products.

Health—and Taste—Benefits

You could be forgiven for thinking that organic goods are always healthier than nonorganic ones. I know that my mom shops fairly indiscriminately, thinking that if something has the word *organic* on the label, then it must be good for her. She's right in the sense that buying this food is a way of minimizing the amount of pesticide residues that she consumes.

At the moment, however, there's only a small amount of evidence linking dietary pesticides with health problems in humans (although there's a lot of information making that connection in animals). We don't really know what the potential toxic effects of eating pesticide residues over a lifetime will be, or the effect of different chemicals combining in a "cocktail." If you want to reduce your consumption of these substances, then go for organic food. That said, the health benefits of eating standard fruits and vegetables are immense, and the risks of eliminating them far outweigh those posed by possible exposure to herbicides and antibiotics.

Do remember, however, that organic doesn't always mean "healthful" in a nutritional sense. For instance, organic-banana chips sound quite healthy, and both the fruit and oil it's fried in are organic—but take a closer look. The manufacturer uses coconut oil, and the bananas absorb a lot of it. Because this oil is rich in total and saturated fats, you'll end up eating a high-total-fat, high-saturated-fat, high-calorie snack. Yes, it's organic, but hardly what's considered healthy. My mother swapped her organic-banana chips for organic bananas instead, and I think she made a good move.

In addition, sometimes organic food can taste better . . . but not always. Organic chicken is one item where I feel there's a big and noticeable taste difference, and the same goes for steak and other meats. With vegetables and fruits, however, it tends to depend on the type of seed used. It does make sense that a tomato allowed to grow at its own natural speed over many weeks, ripening in the sun in nutrient-rich soil, is going to be a lot tastier than one produced at breakneck speed in a greenhouse.

Frequently Asked Questions

Q. Does "natural" mean "organic"?

A. No. These words aren't interchangeable. Truthful claims such as "free range," "hormone-free," and "natural" can appear on food labels, but they don't mean that the product is organic. Only food labeled as such has been certified as meeting organic standards laid down by the USDA.

Q. Can I trust imported organic foods?

A. Domestically, the USDA is working with other governments on this issue, as outlined earlier in this chapter. In addition, the International Federation of Organic Agricultural Movements (IFOAM) is trying to create equivalent standards internationally. It has around 700 international-member organizations in over 100 countries, with its own accrediting body that approves certification bodies in the member countries that reach its own exacting standards. Some supermarkets in the U.S. have signed a commitment to only buy IFOAM-approved organic foods from abroad that meet the USDA NOP standards.

Q. Why is organic food more expensive?

A. The cost is actually coming down, although this isn't always the perception. It's unlikely that organic food will ever be the same price as a supermarket's standard fare. The time, effort, and investment that go into producing it will always set it apart. This isn't to say that organic food should be accessible just to the wealthy. Careful budgeting, including spending less on junk food, could help open the organic market to a wider range of potential customers.

Keep in Mind . . .

Whether organic food is higher in vitamins and minerals hasn't yet been fully established, but we can be sure that it has fewer pesticides and antibiotic residues. It's also environmentally friendly and is produced within the highest possible standards of animal welfare.

Organic food does tend to be more expensive, but costs are coming down. The more people buy, the more items will become available, and the more competitively priced they'll be.

At the other end of the spectrum from the organic goodies we've just discussed is the subject of the next chapter: genetically modified food.

* * *

Chapter 9

Genetically Modified Food

All living things are made up of genetic material called DNA. It's possible to selectively breed both animals and plants to enhance their good points and minimize their less desirable ones, and this practice has been going on in a natural way for thousands of years.

Recently, the process has been dubbed "genetic modification" (GM), which simply means that the genotypes (the normal pattern of DNA) have been slightly altered. This can be done by traditional means, such as avid gardeners interbreeding to create a hybrid with certain characteristics (for example, a new color of rose for their yard). Farmers have also done this for centuries to breed crops that especially suit their land, such as a more robust strain of corn; and it's likely that distinct breeds of dogs wouldn't exist without the GM methods used in animal husbandry.

These days, this general practice can also

involve highly scientific techniques known as "bio-engineering." For example, producers of evening-primrose-oil supplements interbreed species of the plant so that the seeds' oil have the richest supply of omega-6 fatty acids to help people who regularly take their product. The end result is that by adding, deleting, or changing the hereditary traits of agricultural products, the bioengineered crop differs in some way from the original. The modifications may be minor, such as a single mutation that affects one gene, or there may be major alterations that affect many genes. Most, if not all, cultivated-food crops grown today have been genetically modified in some way—but is this a good thing?

"Bioengineering" sounds a little scary to some of us, conjuring up images of "Frankenstein" food. In fact, this is just one of a number of technologies used to create crops. While it's accurate to say that this food has been "genetically modified," some other GM-labeled products are made from plants that have simply been naturally interbred—not grown through the complex methods of bioengineering. Let's take a closer look at the potential benefits and drawbacks involved in the broad scope of this science.

Advantages of Genetically Modified Foods

One argument put forward by those in favor of genetic modification is that by artificially transferring DNA from one organism to another, it's possible to make a crop more resistant to insects or to a fungus that could otherwise destroy it.

GM can solve another common agricultural problem as well, which is that herbicides used to keep weeds under control in fields can also adversely affect the growth of the crops they're intended to protect. Supporters of this new technology point out that by popping a gene into a plant that makes it resistant to specific herbicides, the chemical can then be used without damaging the desirable seedlings. Bioengineering companies also say that in some cases, modifying plants can make them more resistant to attack by natural predators (such as insects), and to diseases caused by infections.

There's also work showing the possibility of making modifications that will enhance nutritional value. For instance, tomatoes have been bred that contain higher amounts of the antioxidant lycopene, which research suggests may help reduce the risk of both heart disease and prostate cancer in men when eaten regularly.

Supporters of this technology also believe that it benefits the food industry when it comes to animals. They assert that by altering genes, livestock can be made to grow more rapidly, to a larger size, or even produce more consumer goods (such as more milk from cows).

Drawbacks of Genetically Modified Foods

For many of us, bioengineering of our food just doesn't "feel" right—there's an instinctive gut reaction that we shouldn't be messing with nature in this way. In reality, the bottom line is that foods that have been genetically modified by bioengineering methods should in theory pose only the same kinds of risks to human health as other foods. Some people, for instance, may be allergic to products containing wheat, bioengineered or otherwise. But does this theory hold true in the real world? Let's take a look at some of the basic issues.

Before a product containing a genetically modified ingredient can be sold to consumers, company scientists must figure out whether there are any new or extra risks that could be attributed to the food or drink. They work with the FDA on this issue to assess the safety of such foods. The actual potential problems are quite complex to understand, but here are two brief points to give you an idea of what could go wrong when genetic modification is used in our food chain:

1. In nature, many factors regulate the expression of a gene. If you take a gene out of its natural environment and drop it in a foreign place—minus these natural controlling factors—the gene may express itself in ways that couldn't have been anticipated.

2. When physically transferring genes, things called "gene promoters" are used, along with "gene markers," which help tell the scientists if material has been successfully transferred. These markers often have bacterial and viral origins, and we don't really know how these will impact health.

Safety Tests

From the tests that have been done so far, we know that bioengineering foods may be a problem for some people, such as those with certain allergies. For instance, if someone has a bad allergy to soy or nut protein, and if those protein genes have been transferred to another food, they may have a reaction to a food that they simply weren't aware contained these genes.

So far, plants have undergone relatively simple changes to their genetic composition through bio-engineering technologies, and it seems as though safety tests have been able to keep abreast of these developments. However, with the increasingly complex compositional changes that are being lined up, new testing technologies will have to be created to keep up with these advances. No scientific evidence exists, but supporters say there's no suggestion that long-term harm (such as higher rates of cancer) may occur from eating such foods.

GM Food Labeling

If you really want to avoid food that's been bioengineered in a way that changes its genetic makeup, then you need to find out from the label which products contain such ingredients—but this isn't always possible. As the law stands, the label only has to state that bioengineering has taken place if the food is "materially different" from the version produced by traditional means. In practice, the phrase describes these circumstances:

- The food differs so much from the original that the common name for it no longer properly describes the product.

- If the product somehow takes on a different use from the original.

- If the genetically engineered version has significantly different nutritional content.

- If the processing it's undergone means that the new food contains a potential allergen other than what you'd normally expect to find based on the item's common name. In this case, the presence of the allergen must be flagged on the label.

If you wish to avoid bioengineering, the kinds of statements to look for on foods include:

- "We don't use ingredients that were produced using biotechnology."
- "This oil is made from soybeans that weren't genetically engineered."
- "Our tomato growers don't plant seeds developed using biotechnology."

Otherwise, the only fail-safe way to avoid foods and drinks that have undergone genetic engineering is to buy organic versions. By law, these can't have been processed in any such way.

Genetically Modified Organism (GMO)

Terms such as "GMO-free" are misleading because most foods don't contain organisms. Seeds and foods such as yogurt that contain microorganisms are exceptions. It's probably best to ignore foods and drinks that declare the absence of genetically modified organisms, since the term doesn't necessarily mean that much.

Frequently Asked Questions

Q. If I want to buy some cheese and it's been produced with genetically modified rennin [the enzyme that makes milk separate into solid curds and watery whey], will the label tell me so?

A. No. The cheese producer doesn't need to tell you that the rennin used was bioengineered because the end product isn't considered "materially different" from the original cheese. Buying organic cheese, however, will guarantee that the rennin hasn't been altered.

Q. How will I know if the milk I'm purchasing has come from cows fed on bioengineered crops?

A. You won't. This also applies to meat (such as lamb and beef) that comes from animals fed on genetically modified crops, as well as eggs laid by chickens given food made from bioengineered plants. Buying organic versions, once again, means that livestock hasn't consumed this type of material.

Keep in Mind . . .

Genetic modification is a relatively new development, so it's almost impossible at this stage to make any absolute pronouncements. The jury is still out on whether or not GM foods will have long-term side effects, and on how harmful or beneficial they might be. At the moment, as you've seen, the only surefire way to avoid bioengineered foods is to buy organic products (see Chapters 6 and 8).

In the next chapter, we'll take a look at another specialized category that revolves around product use, rather than its origin: functional food.

* * *

Chapter 10

Functional Food

These days, it's hard to find a breakfast cereal that doesn't have vitamins and minerals added to it, or an orange juice that hasn't been boosted with an extra nutrient or two. There are fruit smoothies with herbal extracts, and even sweets are proclaiming that they contain added vitamin C.

Tossing vitamins and minerals into food and beverages isn't a completely new thing. In fact, the law requires that certain items have nutrients added. Milk, for example, has vitamins A and D, and similarly, infant formulas must also be fortified with various nutrients to try to make them as similar as possible in composition to breast milk.

These exceptions aside, other fortification is voluntary and is usually done to give the manufacturers something to boast about on their labels, and to make their product different from others on the shelves. These "added value" products are often referred to as "functional foods."

They're usually products that give a health benefit beyond the basic nutrition that they supply.

These items are similar (if not identical) in appearance to conventional products and have the same place in our diets as conventional products. The difference is that the added ingredients they contain have been demonstrated to have a physiological benefit, which may, for instance help reduce the risk of a certain disease.

Currently, the FDA is being very conservative in its approach to how these products are regulated, and consequently, they're subject to the same labeling and safety laws as any other food or drink and have to follow the same guidelines regarding nutrition and health claims (although in certain cases special health claims may be allowed for certain ingredients).

See Chapter 4 for a complete overview of "general and approved" and "qualified" health claims that are permitted, which can help you understand how functional ingredients may be helpful to your health.

Common Added Ingredients

Here are many of the functional ingredients that you may find on labels of common supermarket products.

Plant Stanol and Sterol Esters

Some new types of spreads, yogurts, and yogurt drinks are topped up with substances called "plant stanol" and "plant sterol esters." These natural substances are found in certain plants. They aren't absorbed in the digestive system but pass out undigested in the stool.

Potential health benefits: These have one important action in the digestive system, which is their ability to grab on to cholesterol. They then take hold of it, and both they and the cholesterol get passed out of the body.

Margarine that contains this functional ingredient has gone beyond the role of being a spread for your toast or sandwiches and has taken on the additional role of actively reducing cholesterol. The same is true of yogurts containing these plant stanol and plant sterol esters.

Permitted health claim: Because these kinds of foods have been thoroughly researched and have definitely been shown to lower blood cholesterol in people whose levels are raised, they're allowed to make a specific health claim declaring: "Foods containing at least 0.65 g per serving of vegetable-oil sterol esters, eaten twice a day with meals for a daily total intake of at least 1.3 g as part of a diet low in saturated fat and cholesterol, may reduce the risk of heart disease. A serving of [name of the food] supplies X g of vegetable-oil sterol esters."

Soy Protein

Certain foods, such as breakfast cereals and some cookies, are now having soy protein added to them.

Potential health benefits: There's good evidence that the protein in soy helps lower bad LDL cholesterol; 25 g a day is the amount believed to have this effect. This may in turn help reduce the risk of heart disease. You could just eat lots of foods such as tofu and soy milk, but the enriched products give you added choices.

Permitted health claim: "25 g of soy protein a day, as part of a diet low in saturated fat and cholesterol, may reduce the risk of heart disease. A serving of [name of the food] supplies X g of soy protein."

In order for soy-based foods or drinks to carry this kind of health claim, they must also be low in saturated fat, total fat, and cholesterol. However, there are certain exceptions to this rule, which include foods made from whole soybeans. This is because the whole beans naturally supply 7 g of fat per 100 g (to qualify as "low fat," a food needs to have 3 g or less fat per serving). But if a product is made from whole soybeans and has extra fat added, such as a frozen dinner, then it wouldn't be allowed to carry the health claim after all.

Beta Glucan

Beta glucan is a form of soluble fiber found in oats, oat flour, and oat bran that forms a gel-like substance in the intestines. It can be added to loaves of bread.

Potential health benefits: This gel helps reduce the amount of cholesterol absorbed across the intestinal wall by carrying it out in stools.

Permitted health claim: "Soluble fiber from foods such as [type of food] as part of a diet low in saturated fat and cholesterol may reduce the risk of heart disease. A serving of [type of food] supplies X g of soluble fiber [give its name] necessary per day to have this effect."

Calcium

This mineral is crucial for building and maintaining strong bones, as well as the contraction and relaxation of muscles. It's naturally found in dairy foods such as milk, yogurt, and cheese; oily fish eaten with its bones, such as canned sardines; nuts; sesame seeds; dried fruits; and dark-green leafy vegetables. It's now added to orange juice, mineral water, and breakfast cereals and bars.

Potential health benefits: For people who don't get sufficient calcium from foods naturally rich in this mineral, the functional food can be a helpful addition. The only problem is that some products, such as sugar- and salt-rich breakfast cereals and bars, aren't exactly healthy foods overall. You need to choose carefully when deciding to use calcium-enriched foods and drinks to boost your levels of this mineral.

Permitted health claim: "Regular exercise and a healthy diet with enough calcium helps teens and young adult white and Asian women maintain good bone health and may reduce their high risk of osteoporosis later in life"

To carry this claim, a food must contain 20 percent or more of the Daily Value for calcium. This means that a typical serving must supply at least 200 mg.

Potential Functional Ingredients

The scientific community is continuing to increase its understanding of the potential for functional foods and their role in health. Food-labeling laws may ultimately be altered to take this new information into account. Here are some of the ingredients that may appear in the future in our foods and drinks, which would turn them from regular products into functional foods. These substances aren't currently allowed to have "general and approved" or "qualified" health claims made about their presence.

Dietary Fiber

This would refer to insoluble fiber from wheat bran.

Potential health benefits: Diets rich in insoluble fiber, which passes through the intestines largely undigested, is thought by scientists to reduce the risk of colon cancer.

Potential health claim: May contribute to maintenance of a healthy digestive tract.

Inulin, Fructo-Oligosaccharides, and Polydextrose

These are known as "probiotics." They can be added to breakfast cereals.

Potential health benefits: These are the food sources for the good bacteria in our colons, called "probiotic" bacteria. They're naturally present in whole grains, chicory, onions, garlic, honey, and leeks. They're also in fortified beverages. Because they improve the bacteria count in the colon, they may help boost immunity and improve intestinal health.

Potential health claim: May improve gastrointestinal health; may improve calcium absorption.

Lactobacilli and Bifidobacteria

You can already find bacteria with long, tongue-twisting names (such as Lactobacillus casei Shirota, Lactobacillus GG, Lactobacillus johnsonii, and Lactobacillus casei Immunitas) splashed on labels for yogurts, yogurt drinks, and even fruit drinks. These are another type of probiotic or "good" bacteria.

Potential health benefits: These bacteria avoid digestion and travel down into the colon where they multiply. They help reduce the number of bad, disease-causing bacteria and seem to help boost the immune system. Some research also shows that these good organisms can improve symptoms of irritable bowel syndrome (IBS).

Taking antibiotics can disturb the natural balance of bacteria in the colon. Having probiotics in foods and drinks may help restore this balance, improve digestive health, and boost the immune system.

Potential health claim: May improve gastrointestinal health and systemic immunity.

Omega-3 Fatty Acids

These essential fats are usually found in oily fish such as salmon, mackerel, sardines, anchovies, pilchards, and (to a lesser extent) tuna. Dark-green vegetables; rapeseed, flaxseed, and linseed oils; and walnuts also contain this type of fatty acid. You can now find bread, spreads, and eggs containing omega-3s in the supermarket. They're already allowed a qualified health claim in the context of potentially helping reduce the risk of coronary heart disease, but they may have other extra benefits when added to foods.

Potential health benefits: Research shows them

to be of crucial importance to the development of a baby's brain in the last three months of pregnancy and the first few months of life. A lack has been associated with problems such as dyslexia and hyperactivity in children, and depression in adults. They've also been shown to reduce the risk of blood clotting and to decrease inflammation, helping improve the symptoms of rheumatoid arthritis, psoriasis and Crohn's disease.

Intake of omega-3 essential fats does seem to have fallen during the last century due to a reduced consumption of oily fish. It's estimated that in the West, we now eat only 0.1 g a day—an amount that health experts suggest should be doubled. Increasing our consumption can do no harm and may well be extremely beneficial for both adults and children who don't regularly eat oily fish.

Potential health claim: May reduce risk of coronary heart disease and may contribute to maintenance of mental and visual functions.

Supernutrients

There are thousands of chemicals in plants that are neither vitamins nor minerals, and are commonly described as "supernutrients." Many of these have antioxidant properties and perform a huge variety of roles in plants, from giving them their beautiful colors (such as the blue of blueberries) to helping them naturally fend off predators (such as the bitter-tasting substances in broccoli).

Scientists are learning more and more about their potential health-giving and health-protecting benefits for humans. As research continues, it's possible that you may find supernutrients being added to ordinary foods and drinks to give them additional healthful properties. Here are some that you may have begun to see and some that may come in the future.

Beta-Carotene

This is an orange antioxidant pigment found naturally in carrots, sweet potatoes, mangoes, and apricots. It's also present in dark-green vegetables such as spinach (the darker green pigment chlorophyll masks the orange color).

Potential health benefits: Scientists say that this supernutrient zaps potentially dangerous free radicals, which may damage cells throughout our bodies and could be responsible for triggering cancers.

Beta-carotene is thought to bolster our cells' antioxidant defenses.

Potential health claim: May help reduce the risk of heart disease.

Isoflavones and Lignans

These supernutrients are known as "plant estrogens" and are naturally found in foods such as soy and lentils. They're now being added to products such as bread.

Potential health benefits: Plant estrogens are very similar in shape to human estrogen. Therefore, they have an ability to latch on to estrogen receptors in the body, such as in a woman's breast tissue and in a man's prostate. By doing so, they may reduce the risk of human-estrogen-triggered cancers, such as breast and prostate cancer. They also seem to have a role to play in lowering symptoms of menopause (such as hot flashes) and improving bone health through their imitation of the human hormone.

Although no one really knows for sure, functional foods that are enhanced with these supernutrients probably won't do any harm—and they may well be beneficial. If you're concerned about the effects of products fortified with these particular substances, you can try just eating a lot of soy products, as well as lentils, which are natural sources.

Potential health claim: May contribute to maintenance of bone health, healthy brain and immune function, and for women, maintenance of menopausal health.

Lutein and Zeaxanthin

These are yellow antioxidant pigments found in kale, collard greens, spinach, corn, eggs, and citrus fruits.

Potential health benefits: Research shows that a good intake of these pigments appears to reduce the risk of age-related eye problems, such as helping lower the chances of developing age-related degeneration of the macular lutea, which can cause blindness in later life.

Potential health claim: May help contribute to maintenance of healthy vision.

Lycopene

This is the red antioxidant pigment found in tomatoes and tomato products (such as puree, juice, and soup), as well as in pink grapefruit and watermelon.

Potential health benefits: Scientists have found that in populations where a lot of tomatoes are consumed, the rates of heart disease and prostate cancer appear to be lower than in populations where fewer servings are eaten.

Potential health claim: May contribute to maintenance of prostate health.

Anthocyanidins

These are the beautiful antioxidant pigments found in vegetables and fruits such as red cabbage, berries, cherries, and red grapes.

Potential health benefits: These are associated with improving the strength of the tiny capillary walls in the brain.

Potential health claim: May bolster cellular antioxidant defenses; may contribute to the maintenance of brain function.

Catechins, Epicatechins, and Procyanidins

These strong antioxidants are found in tea, apples, and grapes.

Potential health benefits: Scientists have linked these supernutrients, which all belong to the family called flavanols, to keeping blood vessels in good condition.

Potential health claim: May contribute to the maintenance of heart health.

Flavones

Citrus fruits are the primary sources of these powerful antioxidants, which include hesperetin and limonin.

Potential health benefits: Hesperetin is known for its ability to help vitamin C regenerate, as well as protecting the heart and potentially fighting cancer and viruses.

Potential health claim: Helps neutralize free radicals, which may damage cells, and bolsters cellular antioxidant defenses.

Proanthocyanidins

These are found in cranberries primarily and in smaller amounts in apples, strawberries, grapes, wine, peanuts, cinnamon, and cocoa.

Potential health benefits: Proanthocyanidins have been shown to coat the lining of the urinary tract, creating a "nonstick" surface, which makes it difficult for bacteria to attach themselves and multiply.

Potential health claim: May contribute to maintenance of urinary-tract and heart health.

Quercetin

This antioxidant is found in onions, apples, tea, and broccoli.

Potential health benefits: A high intake of quercetin has been linked with lower rates of stroke and heart disease. It seems to have strong anti-inflammatory and anticancer properties.

Potential health claim: Neutralizes free radicals that may damage cells and bolsters cellular antioxidant defenses.

Sulforaphane

This is a part of cauliflower, broccoli, cabbage, and kale.

Potential health benefits: Sulforaphane has been shown to boost levels of phase-2 enzymes, which grab pollutants and potentially carcinogenic compounds in our bodies and are then flushed out. It's also been shown in laboratory studies to make cancerous cells self-destruct.

Potential health claim: May enhance detoxification of undesirable compounds and bolster cellular antioxidant defenses.

Caffeic and Ferulic Acid

These acids are found in apples, pears, citrus fruits, and some vegetables (such as sweet potatoes).

Potential health benefits: Both appear to have mildly anticancer benefits. Ferulic acid has been found to especially target the cancer-causing compound in tobacco called NNK.

Potential health claim: May bolster cellular antioxidant defenses; may contribute to maintenance of healthy vision and heart health.

Diallyl Sulphide and Allyl Methyl Trisulfide

These tongue-twisting substances appear in garlic, onions, leeks, and scallions.

Potential health benefits: These substances seem to detoxify cancer-causing compounds, as well as maintain good circulation, possibly by keeping blood flowing smoothly and reducing the chances of cholesterol sticking to blood-vessel walls.

Potential health claim: May enhance detoxification of undesirable compounds; may contribute to heart health and good immune function.

Dithiolthiones

These potent compounds are found in broccoli, cabbage, Brussels sprouts, kale, kohlrabi, mustard greens, horseradish, watercress, and turnip greens.

Potential health benefits: They have a range of health-promoting effects in the body, including the potential ability to boost immunity.

Potential health claim: Contribute to maintenance of healthy immune function.

Functional Foods Abroad

Japan

Japan is further ahead in the use of functional ingredients, their development, and the allowance of health claims on labels. Functional foods are a well-established section of this market. Under Japanese law, manufacturers can make specific claims about a food on the label if it's able to remedy a serious health problem. The government makes it quite clear that they support these kinds of added-value, health-promoting foods, in the hopes that by encouraging people to eat and drink them, dietary habits will improve and so cut the cost of health care.

The UK

In the UK, with the exception of the occasional specific claim, most functional foods and drinks that haven't been given special permission must follow the general health-claim guidelines. These are quite similar to those in the U.S.

Are Functional Foods Good for You?

There's general agreement that in some cases the extra nutrients, supernutrients, good (probiotic) bacteria, and standardized herbal extracts put into certain foods and drinks may be beneficial for some people. The key is to get the balance right. What's the point of digging into sweets containing added vitamin C when you could have an orange instead, and get the vitamin without the added sugar?

One concern is that with nutrients being added left and right, you could end up having too much of certain vitamins. For example, pregnant women need to be careful not to have more than 700 mcg a day of vitamin A. Other nutrients (such as vitamin B_6, vitamin D, nicotinic acid, and zinc) can also be toxic if you go above certain limits, so it's best to always err on the side of caution.

Frequently Asked Questions

Q. What other sorts of functional ingredients might we expect to see in the future?

A. It's possible that in the future we may find foods and drinks on the shelves that contain things such as collagen, designed as a nutritional approach to antiaging; or that mushroom extracts may be added to foods to reduce bad breath. Green-tea antioxidants could be put in drinks to help control allergies, along with others intended to reduce eyestrain.

The way forward for functional foods is currently wide open. The category needs strict regulation to ensure that it doesn't go so overboard that there are hardly any real foods left.

Q. If I eat breakfast cereals, fruit juices, and cereal bars—all with added vitamins and minerals—am I at risk of overdosing?

A. It *is* possible to have too much of a good thing—even vitamins and minerals. I'd be very wary of overdoing foods with added nutrients, especially for children. Personally, I think that if you're going to allow any at all, it's worth sticking to just one product category (such as breakfast cereals) and avoiding other items with added vitamins and minerals for the rest of the day.

Q. Are there any really useful functional foods on the market at the moment?

A. Products with plant stanol and plant sterol esters do seem to help reduce cholesterol in people who have raised LDL or "bad" cholesterol. Equally, mineral water and orange juice with added calcium can be useful if dairy sources of this important bone-strengthening mineral are low. I also feel that foods with probiotic "good" bacteria can be useful for strengthening immunity and restoring balance to the colon, especially while taking antibiotics. And foods with omega-3s are great for people who eat little oily fish.

Otherwise, at the moment, I think that functional foods should be treated with caution. I recommend buying and consuming them only if you really know that they'll be of benefit to your health, and that they have no nutritional downsides. Added nutrients being consumed within an implicitly unhealthy food, like a sugary drink or chocolate, aren't a good idea.

Keep in Mind . . .

First, make sure that the functional food is healthy from a holistic perspective. Don't get tempted by an energy-boosting drink that contains guarana, for example, if it's also packed with sugar—you may as well just have a cup of coffee.

Next, consider what you or your family may particularly benefit from. If someone in your household has elevated cholesterol, it's worth considering foods with extras that specifically lower it, such as margarine with plant stanol or sterol esters and products with added soy protein. If you seldom consume any dairy, then drinks with extra calcium may be helpful.

Finally, be selective, because buying functional foods for no particular reason won't necessarily benefit your health—but will definitely increase your food bill. And as for extra ingredients not covered so far, you can find them in the next chapter, which looks at plain old additives.

* * *

Chapter 11

Additives

Mention the word *additive,* and most people conjure up images of food dyes that send children into a whirling frenzy of hyperactivity, but the term covers more than just coloring agents. The list of extras that can be mixed into processed foods is pretty long. They fall into several different categories and are included by manufacturers for a variety of reasons.

Preservatives, for example, are obviously added to protect food from going bad, which means that products can stay on the shelf longer while remaining safe to eat. Other additives make foods taste better, look nicer, stay the proper consistency, or prevent them from separating. In the following pages, you'll find descriptions of 32 types of additives. Let's begin with a look at all the different roles that these substances can play.

Types of Food Additives

Here are the kinds of additives that can be used in food products in the U.S.:

1. Anticaking and free-flow agents are added to finely powdered or crystalline food products such as cake mixes to prevent them from sticking together and "caking" or forming lumps.

2. Antimicrobial agents: As their name suggests, these are added to foods to help stop the growth of microorganisms that would lead to the product spoiling. They include fungistats and mold inhibitors, and are considered to be a type of preservative.

3. Antioxidants help stop foods from going rancid or discoloring through exposure to the atmosphere (a process known as *oxidation*). They're a type of preservative and are used, for example, in margarine to help keep it from going bad.

4. Colors and coloring adjuncts: When a substance is added to a food or drink to give, maintain, or enhance its color, then it falls into this category; this includes additives that stabilize, fix, or retain colors. These are found in everything from cookies and cakes to drinks and margarine.

5. Curing and pickling agents are used to give a unique flavor (and often color) to a food, and usually increase the shelf life, too. They're found in foods such as cooked meats.

6. Dough strengtheners are added to baked goods to make a dough more stable by modifying its starch and gluten content.

7. Drying agents help absorb moisture. Cake mixes are one type of food that may contain these agents.

8. Emulsifiers and emulsifier salts help create a nice, even emulsion in foods such as mayonnaise. In other words, they help keep the oil and water parts of foods in a stable mixture.

9. Enzymes are often added to help along the food-processing technique and improve the quality of the finished product.

10. Firming agents are substances added to help strengthen the supporting tissues in foods, and therefore help prevent collapsing during processing. They can be found in foods such as canned lentils.

11. Flavor enhancers are additives that, as their name indicates, help enhance or modify the original taste of a food without actually lending a special flavor of their own; they can also be used to modify the aroma in a similar way. Monosodium glutamate, which is found in prepared meals and stock cubes, is a flavor enhancer.

12. Flavoring agents and adjuvants impart, or help impart, a taste or aroma in food. These differ from flavor enhancers because they are giving their own qualities to the product, rather than just boosting what's already there.

13. Flour-treating agents: Added to flour at the mill, these substances help improve the flour's color and/or baking qualities. This category includes bleaching agents.

14. Formulation aids can include substances that help bind or fill different ingredients in order to give the right texture to a finished product.

15. Fumigants, as you might expect from their name, are used to help control insects and other pests. They're known as "volatile" substances.

16. Humectants help a product retain moisture. They include antidusting agents and are hygroscopic, which means that they absorb water and stop mold growth. A typical example is the glycerine used in icing on wedding cakes.

17. Leavening agents are used in baked goods to produce or stimulate the production of carbon dioxide to give a light texture. They include yeast, yeast foods, and calcium salts, as well as the baking soda used in making bread.

18. Lubricants and release agents are added to the surface of certain finished products to help prevent things from sticking to them.

19. Nonnutritive sweeteners include substances such as aspartame, which has less than 2 percent of the caloric value of sucrose (table sugar) per equivalent unit of sweetening capacity.

20. Nutrient supplements: This is the term used to describe substances necessary for the body's nutritional and metabolic processes; the category includes vitamins and minerals.

21. Nutritive sweeteners: Unlike nonnutritive sweeteners, which add virtually no calories to products such as diet drinks, members of this category have more than 2 percent of the caloric value of sucrose (table sugar) per equivalent unit of sweetening capacity. Isomalt, sorbitol, and xylitol fall into this group and are used in chewing gum and sugar-free candy.

22. Oxidizing and reducing agents chemically oxidize or reduce another food ingredient, which creates more stable finished products that will go bad less rapidly than they would without the additives.

23. pH control agents: Sometimes manufacturers need to maintain or change the pH (or acidity) of their products. These additives achieve that goal, and include buffers, acids, alkalis, and neutralizing agents. A common example is the citric acid added to lemonade.

24. Processing aids are used during manufacturing to enhance the appeal or function of the end product. This category includes clarifying agents, clouding agents, catalysts, flocculants, filter aids, and crystallization inhibitors. Soft drinks may contain one or more of these.

25. Propellants, aerating agents, and gases: If you buy whipped cream in a canister, it needs a gas to create the force to propel it out of the can. This is known as a *propellant.* These additives also include substances that can reduce the amount of oxygen in contact with the food inside its packaging.

26. Sequestrants: Traces of metals such as iron and copper that occur naturally in food can cause the product to oxidize and go bad prematurely. Sequestrants latch on to these trace metals and make them inactive, thus improving stability and shelf life.

27. Solvents and vehicles are used to help extract or dissolve another substance.

28. Stabilizers and thickeners help manufacturers produce viscous solutions, give their products more body, improve consistency, and stabilize emulsions. This category includes suspending, bodying, setting, jellying, and bulking agents and can be found in everything from ice cream to salad dressings.

29. Surface-active agents modify the surface properties of liquid food components. They include wetting, foaming, and antifoaming agents. The latter can be found in beer and jams.

30. Surface-finishing agents help a product look more palatable by preserving its natural gloss. The category also includes additives capable of preventing discoloration during storage and on the shelf, such as glazes, polishes, and waxes.

31. Synergists are additives that act or react with another ingredient in the food to produce a total effect different or greater than the sum of the effects produced by the individual ingredients.

32. Texturizers, as you'd expect from their name, help affect the appearance or feel of a food that's considered desirable by consumers.

Additive Labeling

As with most food-labeling law, it's in the hands of the FDA as to which additives can be used in foods and drinks. They have a special section of regulations within the Federal Food, Drug, and Cosmetic Act that governs the use of general food additives (the Food Additives Amendment of 1958) and color additives (Color Additives Amendment of 1960).

Additives are listed in the ingredients section of the food label in a variety of ways:

— **Flavors:** If they're natural, they may be listed by their common name or just as the words *flavor, flavoring, natural flavor,* or *natural flavoring.* Artificial flavors must declare themselves as such with the term *artificial flavor.*

— **Colors:** Those certified by the FDA must be listed specifically by their full or abbreviated names in all foods, with the exception of butter, cheese, and ice cream. Mixtures of colors may be listed as "artificial color" followed by a specific list in parentheses, such as: "Ingredients: artificial color (including Yellow 6, Red 40)."

— **Functional additives:** Additives put into a food or drink for a specific functional purpose, including firming agents and emulsifiers, may be declared in the ingredients list in several ways:

- Ingredients: soy lecithin (emulsifier)
- Ingredients: emulsifier (soy lecithin)
- Ingredients: citric acid (acidifier)
- Ingredients: acidifier (citric acid)

— **Preservatives:** The ingredients list must supply the name of the chemical preservative as well as its reason for being there—for instance: "Ingredients: ascorbic acid (to promote color retention)."

Safety Issues

Additives have to be considered safe by the FDA in order to be permitted in foods and drinks. The FDA approval comes with specific and implicit instructions regarding which types of foods each specific additive may be used in, the maximum amounts allowed, and precisely how it should appear on the labels. In addition, a section of the Food Additives Amendment called The Delaney Clause established a zero-tolerance policy toward additives that are found to cause cancer in tests on animals or humans.

To further assure safety, the FDA may require the manufacturer to monitor the substance. In fact, all additives are subject to ongoing safety checks as scientific research continues to advance. The first exceptions to these rules are substances that were given the okay before the 1958 additives amendment.

The only additional exceptions are for ingredients that are officially "Generally Regarded as Safe" (GRAS) by the FDA. For instance, some foods are also used as additives, such as vinegar (which can be used for its preservative actions). Other additives include bromelain (an enzyme that is naturally present in pineapples), which helps tenderize meat; and agar, a natural thickening agent from seaweed. Such substances are GRAS and can be used as additives without special safety precautions.

If additives that haven't been given approval by the FDA are put into foods or drinks, it's considered to be adulteration. This is illegal, and the products would be withdrawn from sale.

In spite of the strict laws governing their usage, some people still feel anxious about the number and types of additives allowed into our food. For example, the Center for Science in the Public Interest doesn't feel 100 percent confident in the approval process used by the FDA. They've created their own guide, which you may want to look at for an alternative view regarding safety and your own usage. You can find it online at **www.cspinet.org/reports/chemcuisine.htm.**

Are Additives a Good or Bad Thing?

The relative merit of additives depends on your individual viewpoint. If you're a food manufacturer, then they obviously tend to be a good thing. Although only a very small proportion of additives used are preservatives, the others—such as flavor enhancers and emulsifiers, anticaking agents, and substances that make products more bulky—are a great advantage. They make it possible to produce an ever-expanding array of brightly colored, tasty foods that can remain on the shelf for long periods of time. Many modern products simply wouldn't exist without the use of additives to create their physical structure, taste, and appearance.

Some shoppers would certainly consider this to be an advantage and would rather have such foods with the additives they implicitly supply. Other consumers are aware that additives may pose health risks, and they actively avoid foods and drinks containing them. If you know that you or a member of your family are intolerant of certain ingredients or suffer bad reactions to some preservatives, then additives aren't such a great thing. Check out the CSPI Website: **www.cspinet.org/reports/chemcuisine.htm**, for a list of the additives most often associated with adverse side effects.

How Can I Minimize My Intake?

Being aware of why and how additives are used in food and drink production allows you to stand back and think objectively about whether you personally want them as part of your diet and life. Once you know the roles they play, you can decide whether you'd prefer your dried apricot to be coated with sulphur dioxide to keep its orange color, or an uncoated version that's dark brown, the real color of dried apricots. It's your choice as to whether you buy plain yogurt and add real strawberries to it or strawberry-flavored yogurt that contains additives to give it a pink color and strawberry taste.

Criticism over such extensive use of additives in

food tends to focus on the fact that some are thought to be linked with adverse reactions, and that they're sometimes used to disguise the use of cheap ingredients. For example, some burgers contain cheap, fatty cuts of meat but are made to look and taste better with red colorings and meat flavorings. No matter how they may look and taste, your body still knows that they're fatty pieces of meat.

If you want to minimize the amount of additives you eat because you instinctively just don't like the idea of swallowing hundreds of added chemicals, then you'll have to go back to basics. This means cutting out all standard processed foods—and by that I mean all prepared meals, cakes, cookies, soft drinks, jam, ketchup, mustard, and so on. You'll have to stick with fresh cuts of organic meat, chicken, and fish, and fresh and frozen vegetables and fruit.

Keep in Mind . . .

It's difficult in this day and age to totally avoid consuming foods and drinks that contain additives. It is, however, possible to minimize the amount you have. The most effective way of doing so is by eating organic food—or simply go back to eating the way your grandparents did, with traditional meals of unprocessed meat with plenty of fresh fruits and vegetables. By cutting back on processed foods, snacks, candy, and store-bought cakes and cookies, you can really reduce your additive load.

Personally, I think that any change you can make to your diet that reduces the reliance on over-processed food is a step in the right direction. I hope that the information in this book has given you the building blocks for a greater understanding of what you're really eating so that you can make informed choices each and every day.

* * *

Resource Guide

Much of the information in the book came from the following references:

The Food Labeling Regulations 1996, No. 1499, HMSO

The Food Labeling (Amendment) (No. 2) Regulations 1999, No. 1483, The Stationery Office

Code of Practice on Health Claims on Foods. Joint Health Claims Initiative

Food Additives Legislation Guidance Notes. Food Standards Agency, March 2002

Nutrition Labeling and Health Claims, British Nutrition Foundation, September 2002

Proposal for a Regulation of the European Parliament and of the Council on nutrition and health claims made on foods. 2003/0165 (COD), OJEC

Guidance Notes on Nutrition Labeling, MAFF 1999

The Genetically Modified & Novel Foods (Labeling) (England) Regulations 2000, The Stationery Office

"This Product May Contain Nuts" Voluntary Labeling Guidelines for Food Allergens and Gluten, Institute of Grocery Distribution, May 2000

Marketing Food to Kids, The Consumer Association, August 2003

Honest Labeling Campaign, The Consumer Association

Food Label—The Hidden Truth, The Consumer Association, July 2002

Useful Contacts

Food Labeling Regulations
www.lhmso.gov.uk/si/si1996/uksi_1996/499_en_l.htm

Food Standards Agency
www.foodstandards.gov.uk

The Consumer Association
2 Marylebone Road, London, NW1 4DF. 020 7770 7612
www.which.net/campaigns/food

British Nutrition Foundation
High Holborn House, 52-54 High Holborn, London,
WC1V 6RQ. 020 7404 6504
postbox@nutrition.org.uk

The Institute of Grocery Distribution
Grange Lane, Letchmore Heath, Watford, Herts,
WD2 8DQ. 01923 857141
www.igd.com

Coeliac UK
PO Box, No. 220, High Wycombe, Bucks, HP11 2HY.
01494 437278
www.coeliac.co.uk

The Vegetarian Society
Parkdale, Dunham Road, Altrincham, Cheshire,
WA14 4QG. 0161 925 2000
www.vegsoc.org

The Vegan Society
Donald Watson House, 7 Battle Road, St Leonards-
on-Sea, East Sussex, TN3 7AA. 01424 427393
www.vegansociety.com

The Soil Association
Bristol House, 40-56 Victoria Street, Bristol, BS1 6BY.
0117 929 0661
www.soilassociation.org

The National Osteoporosis Society
Camerton, Bath, BA2 OPJ. 01761 471771
www.nos.org.uk

Diabetes UK
10 Parkway, London, NW1 7AA. 020 7424 1000
www.diabetes.org.uk

HEART UK
7 North Road, Maidenhead, Berkshire, SL6 1PE.
01628 628638

Baby Organix
www.babyorganix.co.uk

Fair Trade
www.fairtrade.org.uk/products.htm

Information on Additives

For information on artificial sweeteners, enzymes
and flavorings, please contact:
stephen.knight@foodstandards.gsi.gov.uk
Phone 020 7276 8583

For information on all other additives, please contact:
andy.furmage@foodstandards.gsi.gov.uk
Phone 020 7276 8570

* * *

Acknowledgments

My heartfelt thanks for helping me make this book possible go to my friend, nutritionist, and registered dietitian, Rani Beranbaum. Randi went to great lengths to provide me with research material. Without her dedication to the cause, it would not have been possible.

I would also like to thank Randi for reading the manuscript. Thank you so much; you have given me the confidence to make this project happen. Randi is one of the most accomplished dietitians working in the media in America, and I am honored that she worked with me on this project.

I would also like to thank the wonderful Hay House team. Thank you, Reid, for deciding to let me write this book, and to Jill Kramer and Tricia Breidenthal for working so hard to make it happen.

* * *

About the Author

Amanda Ursell, a native of the UK, is a member of the British Dietetic Society and Nutrition Society, a Visiting Fellow of Oxford Brookes University in the UK, and a Fellow of the Royal Society of Health. Amanda recieved a B.Sc in Nutrition from King's College London, and went on to acquire a diploma in dietetics. Having worked in hospitals as a dietitian, she went on to pursue a career in the media, writing and broadcasting extensively both in the UK and in America, where she had a column in the *L.A. Times.* Voted Health Professional of the Year and Health Journalist of the Year, Amanda has a passion for communicating the messages of nutrition in a simple, clear, and conscise way that is both understandable, and most important, as she describes, "is actually doable."

* * *

Randi Beranbaum, MS, RD, received at B.Ssc in nutrition and a BA in women's studies from the University of Maryland, College Park, and a dual master's degree in clinical nutrition and nutrition communications from Tufts University. A registered dietitian, she's the managing editor of *Nutrition Today,* a peer-reviewed journal that publishes articles by leading nutritionists and scientists who endorse scientifically sound food, diet, and nutritional practices.

Randi has appeared on local Boston and national television shows including CNN and *Wall Street Week,* and has written and commented widely on nutrition and health throughout the media. She has worked with scientific boards nationally and internationally including the USDA, NIH, National Academy of Sciences, Institute of Medicine, and WHO.

* * *